Fast ASP.NET Websites

Fast ASP.NET Websites

DEAN ALAN HUME

MANNING

SHELTER ISLAND

For Emily — ngiyakuthanda

For online information and ordering of this and other Manning books, please visit
www.manning.com. The publisher offers discounts on this book when ordered in quantity.
For more information, please contact

Special Sales Department
Manning Publications Co.
20 Baldwin Road
PO Box 261
Shelter Island, NY 11964
Email: orders@manning.com

 Manning Publications Co.
20 Baldwin Road

PO Box 261
Shelter Island, NY 11964

Development editor: Jennifer Stout
Technical proofreader: Adam West
Copyeditor: Laura Cheu
Proofreader: Elizabeth Martin
Typesetter: Dennis Dalinnik
Cover designer: Marija Tudor

ISBN: 9781617291258
Printed in the United States of America
1 2 3 4 5 6 7 8 9 10 – MAL – 19 18 17 16 15 14 13

contents

preface

Ever since I began building websites, I've been interested in learning how to make them more efficient. It's a great feeling when you transform a slow website into a finely tuned engine that makes people say "Wow!" In my pursuit to improve my websites' performance, I've trawled the net and spent long hours trying to find the best techniques. Technology is constantly developing and improving, and developers are finding newer and ever more ingenious ways of speeding up their sites.

If you're a developer who is new to coding and website performance, the plethora of resources can be quite overwhelming. Until I wrote *Fast ASP.Net Websites*, I hadn't seen a book that teaches the ASP.NET developer the exact formula, in a step-by-step process, how to shave seconds off their page load times and drastically improve the performance of their websites.

I hope you agree this is that book.

acknowledgments

Until now I never thought about all the research and background work that goes into writing a technical book. This book would definitely not have been possible without the help of many people.

Most importantly, I want to thank my partner Emily for her encouragement and for sticking with me through all the early mornings and weekends it took to finish this book. Every time my alarm went off, you never complained, not even once. Thank you for all your support!

Sincere thanks to Jennifer Stout at Manning Publications for being the best development editor...ever. Your cheerful attitude and brilliant work were instrumental in the evolution of this book. Thank you for always listening to my ideas and being so efficient. Thanks to Michael Stephens for believing in me and in the idea I had for this book. You guided me through each step of the process and this book wouldn't have been possible without your advice! Thanks to Candace Gillhoolley for your help with the marketing of this book and to Rebecca Rinehart for working with me on my idea for the book cover. Many thanks also to everyone on the Manning production team for guiding me through the process and bringing the book to press.

Special thanks to Sam Saffron for helping me review the MiniProfiler content. Sam was one of the creators of MiniProfiler and helped me, even though he and his wife had a new baby on the way, and he was in the process of launching a new website!

I am also grateful to all the reviewers who helped shape and improve the manuscript during its development: Bryn Keller, Danylo Kizyma, Ivo Štimac, James Berkenbile,

Jason Hales, Jeff Smith, Mark Sponsler, Michael Roberts, Onofrio Panzarino, and Wyatt Barnett.

Special thanks to Robin Osborne and Tim Clarke for their reviewing help, and to Adam West for his technical proofread of the final manuscript.

I would like to thank my family for their encouragement throughout the writing process. You have been fantastic!

Finally, thank *you* for purchasing this book. I hope you enjoy reading it as much as I enjoyed writing it. I hope you will learn valuable techniques you can use and apply to all your websites.

Let's make the web faster!

about this book

This book is designed to allow you, as a developer, to get the best performance out of your websites. This book delivers details, best practices, caveats, tips, and tricks to improve the performance of your websites and reduce the load times of your web pages.

How to use this book

Every new chapter in this book is intended to teach the reader a new web performance concept. As you follow along with each chapter, and open the accompanying source code, you will be able to follow the steps provided to improve the performance of the sample website. Each chapter in the book is also designed to work as a standalone concept; that is, you can chose a chapter and apply just that technique and you will improve your website. As we progress through the chapters, we will be constantly improving the sample website and each technique will take the sample website closer to performance nirvana.

Who should read this book

This book is for web developers who are looking to improve the performance of their web pages. It is also for developers who are looking to dive a little deeper into web development and understand the page lifecycle that is happening as a user loads their website. This book covers fundamental techniques that are applicable to web pages regardless of the programming language. The techniques that are covered are generally universal, but aimed toward the ASP.NET website developer.

Roadmap

Part 1 "Defining performance" teaches you the valuable skills you need to understand in order to begin improving the performance of your website. It explains the importance of focusing on the front-end code in order to achieve the biggest and most scalable gains.

Chapter 1 explains the value and benefits that optimizing your websites will bring. It also shows you the steps you'll need to take in order to optimize your websites by using the Performance Cycle.

Chapter 2 focuses on the basics of HTTP so you understand the processes that take place under the hood. The chapter then shows you the essential tips and tools you'll need in order to interpret performance charts when you're profiling your website. You'll then look at the different profiling tools that you'll be using throughout this book.

Part 2 "General performance best practices" is where the real work begins. You'll start to investigate and apply individual techniques to improve the performance of your web applications.

Chapter 3 covers compression and why you should use it. After going through the different types of compression, you'll look at the Surf Store application used throughout this book. You'll then apply compression to the sample application and compare the difference in page sizes.

Chapter 4 looks at HTTP caching and shows how you can use it to improve the performance of your web applications. The chapter also shows you how to apply output caching to your ASP.NET projects.

Chapter 5 explains the new bundling and minifying features built into ASP.NET 4.5. You'll then run through examples and apply them to the Surf Store application.

Chapter 6 dives a little deeper into web performance and offers HTML optimization tips and techniques you can apply to your web pages. It also explains the performance benefits HTML5 can bring, as well as ways to integrate these HTML5 techniques into your web pages.

Chapter 7 discusses the importance of image optimization and how it can significantly reduce the weight of your web pages. This chapter looks at the different image optimization tools available and shows you how to use them. The chapter discusses the benefits data URIs can bring and walks you through an end-to-end example that demonstrates how you can apply data URIs to an ASP.NET application.

Chapter 8 discusses ETags and explains their usage on the web today. It explores whether you should or shouldn't be using them in your web application and runs through an example that demonstrates how to remove ETags from your application.

Chapter 9 focuses on Content Delivery Networks (CDNs) and the benefits they can bring in terms of speed and performance. It teaches you how to build a simple HTML helper that you can use in your ASP.NET development when dealing with CDNs. This technique can help you save money and bandwidth expenses when dealing with CDNs in a development environment.

Part 3 "ASP.NET-specific techniques" starts to shift focus slightly and looks at ASP.NET optimization techniques that are based on server-side code.

Chapter 10 teaches you how to tweak your ASP.NET MVC applications to squeeze precious milliseconds out of your page load time. The chapter shows you how to apply a profiler called MiniProfiler to your MVC application and use it to pinpoint bottlenecks in your application.

Chapter 11 shows simple techniques you can use to improve the performance of your ASP.NET Web Forms applications, how to apply MiniProfiler to your ASP.NET Web Forms application, and how to identify any bottlenecks in your code.

Chapter 12, the final chapter, discusses the importance of server-side data caching. It teaches you how to apply the features built into the System.Runtime.Caching namespace and illustrates an end-to-end example, showing data caching in action. The chapter reviews the progress you've made and compares the Surf Store application before and after we made improvements. The speed differences between the applications are astonishing!

Code conventions and downloads

All source code in the book is in a `fixed-width font`, which sets if off from the surrounding text. In many listings, the code is annotated to point out the key concepts. We have tried to format the code so that it fits within the available space in the book by adding line breaks and using indentation carefully. Sometimes, however, very long lines include line-continuation markers. Code examples appear throughout this book. Long listings appear under clear listing headers; shorter listings appear between lines of text or in an illustration.

Throughout this book, I make use of C#, JavaScript, CSS, and HTML as much as possible. I am a fan of both ASP.NET Web Forms and ASP.NET MVC, and each chapter includes sample code for both frameworks. This allows you to choose either framework and still learn and apply the same techniques.

All of the sample code is available for download on the Github website at https://github.com/deanhume/FastASPNetWebsites as well as from the publisher's website at www.manning.com/FastASP.NETWebsites. Each chapter has its own source code that you should be able to fire up and begin working on immediately. There is no setup involved.

Software requirements

In order to run the code samples that are provided in this book, you will need a copy of Visual Studio 2012. You can use either Visual Studio Express 2012, which is a free download on the Microsoft website, or the full version of Visual Studio 2012. The source code will only work with versions of Visual Studio 2012 and not previous versions as there are some newer features in Visual Studio 2012 that have been built to improve the performance of web pages.

You will also need a copy of either the Yahoo! YSlow tool or the Google PageSpeed tool to profile the sample web pages in this book. These two tools are both free and work with most modern browsers. You will need to check with the vendors to find out which browsers they are compatible with.

Author Online

The purchase of *Fast ASP.NET Websites* includes free access to a private web forum run by Manning Publications where you can make comments about the book, ask technical questions, and receive help from the author and other users. To access the forum and subscribe to it, visit www.manning.com/FastASP.NETWebsites. This page provides information on how to get on the forum once you are registered, what kind of help is available, and the rules of conduct on the forum.

Manning's commitment to our readers is to provide a venue where a meaningful dialogue between individual readers and between readers and the author can take place. It is not a commitment to any specific amount of participation on the part of the author, whose contribution to the forum remains voluntary (and unpaid). Let your voice be heard, and keep the author on his toes!

About the cover illustration

The figure on the cover of *Fast ASP.NET Websites* is captioned "African Warrior." The illustration is taken from a Spanish compendium of regional dress customs first published in Madrid in 1799. The book's title page states:

> *Coleccion general de los Trages que usan actualmente todas las Nacionas del Mundo desubierto, dibujados y grabados con la mayor exactitud por R.M.V.A.R. Obra muy util y en special para los que tienen la del viajero universal.*

Which we translate, as literally as possible, thus:

> *General collection of costumes currently used in the nations of the known world, designed and printed with great exactitude by R.M.V.A.R. This work is very useful especially for those who hold themselves to be universal travelers.*

Although nothing is known of the designers, engravers, and workers who colored this illustration by hand, the "exactitude" of their execution is evident in this drawing. The "African Warrior" is just one of many figures in this colorful collection. Their diversity speaks vividly of the uniqueness and individuality of costumes from different countries around the world just 200 years ago.

We at Manning celebrate the inventiveness, the initiative, and the fun of the computer business with book covers based on the rich diversity of life of two centuries ago brought back to life by the pictures from this collection.

Part 1

Defining performance

The key to improving the performance of your websites is understanding how web pages work. These first two chapters teach the skills that you, the developer, will need to master when improving the performance of your web pages, and the tools you will use to create performance charts.

You'll begin (chapter 1) by learning about the importance of delivering fast web pages to your users and the impact that slower web pages can have on modern businesses. In chapter 2, you'll learn about the performance cycle and how to use this technique to take a step-by-step approach to improving web page performance.

Throughout this book there is a strong emphasis on the front end of a website and in these chapters you learn why it is important to start with the front end when aiming to improve performance. The Performance Golden Rule states that developers should *"optimize front-end performance first, because that's where 80% or more of the end-user response time is spent."* This rule is the basis for the majority of this book.

High-speed websites

In South Africa, the Zulu have a proverb: "Even a small ant can hurt the mighty elephant." Many animals are unable to harm the thick skin of the elephant, but just one ant can crawl into its trunk and cause chaos.

Have you ever opened a website and experienced a long wait (think slow, plodding elephant), waiting for all of the elements on the page to load? As you are waiting, imagine what an army of small improvements could do to make your website faster. Within the wider open source community, there are myriad books about web page performance. But in the .NET community, this remains an evolving area with much of the knowledge scattered about the internet. In this book, I hope to give you tools and tricks you can use to improve the speed of your .NET website, one step at a time.

Starting with the early versions of ASP.NET, there has always been a focus on developer productivity. Unfortunately, with this productivity came elements of the .NET framework that you might not have needed in your application. When you used earlier versions of ASP.NET, you got the whole stack, which included drag-and-drop controls, ViewState, server controls, and clunky HTML. Fortunately, the latest versions of ASP.NET put the focus on simplicity and getting your web framework to work just the way you want. In this book, you'll look at the latest ASP.NET tools (ASP.NET MVC, ASP.NET Web Forms, and IIS) and use them to adjust and tweak your website's code to provide your users with a responsive, high-performance website that runs smoothly. Internet Information Services (IIS) is an integral part of the Windows Server family of products and is one of the most popular servers for hosting websites. You'll be using it to fine tune websites and optimize the way the server returns data to a browser. You'll also look at a sample e-commerce website in both ASP.NET Web Forms and ASP.NET MVC and take it from slow to extremely high speed. You'll create a sample application called Surf Store, which you'll build and improve upon in each chapter. This gradual progression will also help you gain the understanding that you need to create fast ASP.NET websites.

In this first chapter, we'll take a general look at the importance of website speed and the negative impact a slow website can have. In particular, we'll focus on the Performance Golden Rule and how it can make a compelling case for optimization.

1.1 Why optimize?

Steve Souders, the head performance engineer at Google, coined the term the Performance Golden Rule in his book *High Performance Web Sites* (O'Reilly Media, 2007). In it he states that developers should "optimize front-end performance first, because that's where 80% or more of the end-user response time is spent. "

When you first picked up this book and browsed through the table of contents, you may have noticed that a lot of emphasis is placed on front-end techniques (HTML, images, and static files) and not specifically on server-side code optimizations. When I began looking into website performance, I was shocked to discover that the biggest gains I could make were on the front end.

The key to faster websites is to place your focus on improving front-end performance. It has been proven to work and has allowed developers around the world to boost their websites' performance time and time again. According to the Yahoo! YDN blog, more than 50 teams at Yahoo! have reduced their end-user response times by at least 25%. This is a sizeable increase.

Throughout this book, we'll refer to the Performance Golden Rule, because it is the basis for improving website performance. In the following chapters, you'll learn more about the Performance Golden Rule and why it's important. Beyond improving performance, fine tuning the front end of a website has proven benefits in other areas as well.

1.2 The financial impact

Let's start with the money aspect of web page optimization. Depending on your website hosting solution, you may be paying for the bandwidth associated with your site.

Every file downloaded when a user loads your web pages means more bandwidth used. By reducing the amount of bandwidth and number of requests served from your website, you essentially save yourself or your company money.

1.2.1 The business impact

The financial penalty of slow bandwidth is the tip of the iceberg; the business impact of a slow web page can be drastic. Users are becoming more and more accustomed to speedy web pages. Because connection speeds are faster and hardware is better than ever, users expect a certain level of perceived speed when they access a web page. When they don't perceive that speed, they look elsewhere, meaning that you might lose their business.

As more and more people all over the world shop online, they associate the speed of a website with the trust they have for it. If your site is extremely slow, it won't instill confidence. Again, no confidence, lost business.

In a consumer survey conducted by Gomez,[1] nearly one-third (32%) of consumers reported that they abandon slow sites that have between a 1 to 5 second delay.

As a developer, you may not believe that site speed plays such an important role in the way your organization and website are perceived by your users. But in order to test how users respond to different web page timings, Google purposely injected latency into its web pages and found that slowing down the search results page by 100 to 400 milliseconds had a measurable impact: the number of searches per user declined by 0.2% to 0.6%.

Similarly, when the Google Maps home page was reduced in size from 100 KB to 70-80 KB, traffic went up 10% in the first week and an additional 25% in the following three weeks (*Farber 2006*).[2] Other major online players found similar results when they optimized their websites.

1.2.2 The search engine ranking impact

Google's search engine team places emphasis on the speed of a website and how it affects search rankings. Google now includes site speed, an attribute that reflects how quickly a website responds to web requests. Google strongly encourages web developers to begin looking at their site speed and ways in which they can improve it. If you have invested heavily in search engine optimization (SEO), you might find it disheartening if all of your hard work is negatively affected by a slow website that slips down the search rankings.

---

[1] "Why Web Performance Matters: Is Your Site Driving Customers Away?" Gomez, the web performance division of Compuware, whitepaper, copyright 2010, http://mng.bz/tOq5.

[2] "The Psychology of Web Performance," WebSiteOptimization.com, May 30, 2008, http://www.websiteoptimization.com/speed/tweak/psychology-web-performance/.

1.2.3   *The mobile user impact*

Mobile internet usage is increasing dramatically as many mobile users turn to their phones, tablets, and other mobile devices to browse internet sites and get the information they need while on the go. Most mobile providers use 3G technology, which can be prone to wildly varying speeds depending on many factors. 4G is starting to gain traction, yet as developers, we still need to consider slower connections. Even though mobile networks are becoming faster, every millisecond counts! All techniques you'll learn in this book will ensure that mobile users also benefit. Users who browse your website via a mobile device may be paying for their internet usage, so every download you save them when they open up a web page will also go into their back pockets—it's a win-win situation.

1.2.4   *The environmental impact*

Your organization may be considering its green credentials. You'll be surprised to know that any changes you make that improve the performance of your website will also improve your organization's carbon footprint. Web servers require electricity and consume power in order to service the many requests that users make to a website. Imagine if you could cut down on the number of web requests made to your servers. That would mean less traffic for the server, which would mean the server wouldn't have to work as hard to process requests. Some companies may also be running multiple servers to load balance a website. If you cut down on the server load, you might not even need that extra server!

1.3   *How to optimize*

It may seem like an overwhelming task, but the overall process of improving your website's load times and performance can be broken down into four key stages. The performance cycle shown in figure 1.1 is a summary of the entire journey of the

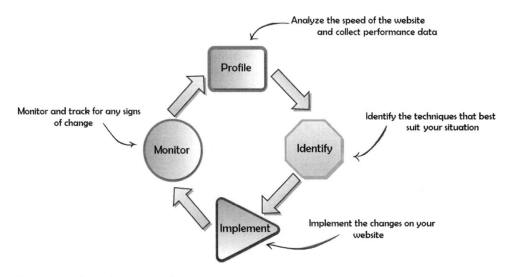

Figure 1.1   The performance cycle

website-improvement process. Its four stages act as a guide that can be applied to any website, regardless of the specific rules and techniques you apply, helping you realize performance potential and faster load times.

A website rarely stays the same for long—it evolves and grows as business expands. These four stages are useful to refer to if you get stuck or are unsure of the next step in the cycle.

1 Profile your website, analyzing it so you can understand where the performance issues are and why they are there.
2 Identify appropriate techniques, learning what best suits your situation and how you can enhance your website's speed.
3 Implement changes, having determined which techniques best suit your website.
4 Monitor your site, tracking for any signs of decreased speed.

1.3.1   Profile

In chapter 2, we'll run through some free tools you can use to effectively profile your website. These tools do the hard work for you by producing charts and results that clearly show where your website can be improved. They pick up obvious and sometimes not-so-obvious areas for improvement. With the results from the profiling tools, learning to read the signs will become a lot easier. Problem solving involves more than simply reproducing behavior—it involves insight.

Before you begin applying the changes, take a snapshot of the website's performance profile to help you see how the improvements you make affect your website. In chapter 2, we'll discuss ways in which you can use performance and waterfall charts to create snapshots of your site as it currently stands; the snapshot can also be used as a benchmark along the way. The satisfaction that you gain from comparing the optimized results to the original results can be very rewarding. Not to mention that these results can be used to impress your boss! You may need to justify spending your time on improving website performance, and what better way to do so than by showing proven results?

1.3.2   Identify

With the results from profiling, you can identify areas that need improvement. With more and more practice, you'll become better at reading the charts and recognizing areas that require attention. You may find that all the techniques that we run through in this book are applicable to your situation, but the results of your analysis might reveal that you need to apply only a few.

1.3.3   Implement

The next step of the improvement process involves implementing the changes to your website. Chapters 3-12 will guide you through this step by step, with each chapter taking a sample website that has a poor performance rating and showing you how to optimize and improve its speed. By the end of the book, you'll have taken this slow sample site and made it a high-caliber website.

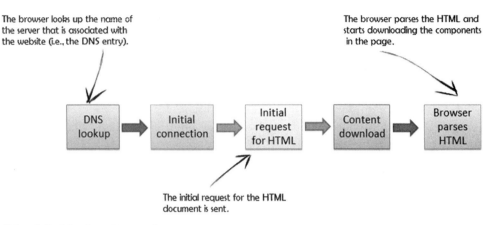

The browser looks up the name of the server that is associated with the website (i.e., the DNS entry).

The browser parses the HTML and starts downloading the components in the page.

The initial request for the HTML document is sent.

Figure 1.2   A basic page request

1.3.4   *Monitor*

The final step in the improvement process is monitoring your website. Once you have made the changes, your site should be stable and remain optimized. But as your site grows, you may find yourself adding new functionality and features. This inevitably leads to more page components, which could cause degradation in page speed. Only by monitoring your site will you be able to maintain this optimized level of performance.

The four-step cycle begins again as a new cycle.

1.4   *Where to optimize*

To improve your website's performance, you must understand where your users spend most of their time waiting for resources to be downloaded. A basic page request is shown in figure 1.2.

In the figure, notice how the content download and the browser parsing the HTML are the last, but most important, parts of the request. The browser parsing the HTML is important because it needs to download enough resources to render the page. To help you visualize how the content download is split, figure 1.3 summarizes the average bytes per page, based on an evaluation of over 250,000 URLs.

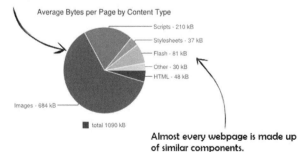

These statistics are run across a set of over 250,000 URLs.

Average Bytes per Page by Content Type

Scripts - 210 kB
Stylesheets - 37 kB
Flash - 81 kB
Other - 30 kB
HTML - 48 kB
Images - 684 kB
total 1090 kB

Almost every webpage is made up of similar components.

Figure 1.3   Average bytes per page by content type (source: httparchive.org). The 250,000 URLs that produce this chart are made up by a large percentage of www.alexa.com's top websites, as well as additional user-submitted websites.

As you can see in figure 1.3, you can see that the HTML document is a very small percentage of the overall download. Surprisingly, users spend most of their time waiting for the other components to download!

As a back-end developer, you probably think the first place to optimize your website is deep in the server-side code. This may include optimizing code or indexing the database. Instead, you need to start thinking about scalability and how quickly a website responds on its first load and even its second, third, and so on. Web page speed has less to do with server-side code and more to do with the components that make up the page. The HTML document is a small percentage of the total response time, and the components are the bulk of the page load. If you look at these components and find ways to improve the download time, these are the areas in which you can make the biggest gains.

1.5 The Performance Golden Rule

Going back to the Performance Golden Rule, as developers, we have to keep in mind what Steve Souders wrote (in *High Performance Web Sites*): we should "optimize front-end performance first, because that's where 80% or more of the end-user response time is spent." Using this rule, you can deduce that if 80% of the download time is spent on the front end, and you cut that in half, you reduce response times by 40%. If you cut the back-end performance in half, you gain only a 10% increase in response times. It almost seems like a no-brainer!

From a business point of view, the resources and skills required to optimize back-end code might require a skilled developer, cost more money, and take longer. Changing back-end code may require rearchitecture of that code, expensive profiling tools, and micro-optimizations. The techniques we cover beginning in chapter 3 are proven to work and can be applied across all web pages on a website with great results.

In figure 1.3, you saw that HTML makes up a very small proportion of the components in a web page. If you refer to the Performance Golden Rule and think again that 80% of user time is spent on page downloads, it becomes obvious where you need to look first! Imagine spending all your time micro-optimizing the server-side code and only making very small gains in speed, whereas you see a huge payoff immediately if you concentrate your efforts on the front end.

That said, although front-end optimization will give you the biggest gains and speed up your website significantly, you might still have room for improvement on the back end of your website. In chapters 10-12 we'll look into ways to help you squeeze those last precious milliseconds out of your website by optimizing the back-end code.

1.6 Summary

As a web developer, you hold tremendous power and responsibility in your hands. Instead of providing your users with an average website, you have the ability to give them that something extra. In this chapter, you've seen that you can make a major difference to your users' experience with simple and basic changes.

In the open source community, there is a growing buzz and excitement around web page performance. The advantages of serving a fast, responsive web page include reduced data traffic costs, increased business revenue, more website conversions, improved reputation, and more time for your users to spend on your site. In addition, optimizing your site's performance can be extremely fun!

In the next chapter, you'll begin learning about the basics of HTTP as well as essential tips and tools for interpreting performance charts. Chapter 2 will give you a solid introduction to web page performance.

First steps toward
a faster website

This chapter runs through the basic tools and skills that you need to know in order to start analyzing your site. You're going to start by learning the basics of HTTP and understanding HTTP requests and responses. You'll also run through performance charts and the tools you can use to create them. By the time you're finished with this chapter, you'll be able to dive straight into coding.

2.1 The basics of HTTP

HTTP, the foundation of all communication on the web, allows browsers and servers to communicate with each other using a request-and-response communication system. HTTP, in the most simple terms, is like a conversation: one person is the browser requesting information, and the other is the server, responding with a result. You (the browser) then interpret the response and act accordingly.

In general, the client always initiates the conversation and the server replies. These HTTP requests and responses contain data that is readable to the human eye, which makes it easy to follow and understand. Most modern browsers come with a set of free tools that enable you to monitor these messages easily.

HTTP messages are made up of a header and a body. The HTTP header contains important data about the client browser, the requested page, and more. It's transmitted in a key/value pair format and is the core part of an HTTP message. Then, in the most basic type of HTTP request, the HTTP message body will contain data being sent to the server. In a request, this is where user-entered data or uploaded files are sent to the server.

Each HTTP request also contains an HTTP verb that tells the server what to do with the data being sent across. You may be familiar with the two most common verbs— GET and POST. They often appear in the HTML action form attributes.

GET is used to request a resource without expecting to change that resource (for example, loading a website's homepage). POST is used to submit data to the resource, which is then updated (for example, submitting your details when changing your user preferences on a website).

2.1.1 Understanding an HTTP GET request

The most common type of HTTP request is GET. Every time you type a URL in your browser and hit return, the action fires off a GET request. Figure 2.1 shows a typical GET request. I have used one of the built-in browser tools that we're going to cover later in this chapter to view its internal contents.

The information inside an HTTP request is full of useful details; it's up to you to understand exactly what is happening.

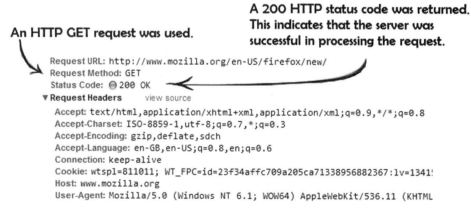

Figure 2.1   An HTTP GET request

In figure 2.1, you'll notice a typical HTTP request to www.mozilla.org.

- The Request Method is listed as a GET, and the Status Code is 200, which means it was successful.
- The Accept header field tells the server which content types are acceptable. In this case, the browser is accepting HTML. The browser also tells the server it supports other content types in case the server doesn't support the first one it asks for. The string containing multiple content types is chained together for efficiency, meaning that the browser doesn't have to request multiple content types one at a time if the first request fails. The Accept-Charset tells the server which character encoding is acceptable (such as ASCII, UTF-8, etc.) For this request, it is ISO-8859-1, UTF-8.
- In the field Accept-Encoding, the browser is letting the server know that it supports Gzip, Deflate, and SDCH compression types. If the data the server sends back is compressed, it will understand how to decompress it and display it to the user. We'll cover compression in chapter 3.
- The browser uses the Accept-Language field to tell the server which languages it can use to respond. In this case it can respond in en-GB and en-US.
- The Connection field tells the server what type of connection the user-agent would prefer. In this request, the browser has asked for a keep-alive connection type.
- The User-Agent field is a text string that browsers and devices use to identify themselves for tracking and other purposes.

2.1.2 Understanding an HTTP GET response

After you've made the HTTP request to www.mozilla.org as shown in figure 2.1, the server replies with an HTTP response.

From the request shown in figure 2.2, you can see the following:

- The server tells the browser that this component can be cached. In this case it's using the Cache-Control field and notifying the browser that it can be cached for 600 seconds. All Cache-Control timings are measured in seconds.

The server has indicated that the response is compressed using GZIP.

▼ Response Headers   view source
Cache-Control: max-age=600   **The content expires in ten minutes.**
Connection: Keep-Alive
Content-Encoding: gzip
Content-Type: text/html; charset=utf-8
Date: Thu, 12 Jul 2012 04:29:54 GMT
Expires: Thu, 12 Jul 2012 04:39:54 GMT
Keep-Alive: timeout=5, max=999
Server: Apache
Transfer-Encoding: chunked
Vary: Accept-Encoding

Figure 2.2 An HTTP GET response

- The Connection field shows Keep-Alive is supported.
- The Keep-Alive field tells the browser which connection limits it supports (time-outs and max connection time).
- The Content-Encoding field tells the browser that the server is sending data back that's encoded with Gzip. Now the browser can decompress that data with the appropriate coding. You'll look at compression more closely in chapter 3.
- The component's Content-Type is text/html.
- The Date field tells the browser the date it was processed so it can cache it if necessary.
- The Expires field tells the browser how long it's allowed to keep the component. The Expires field is a date and time in the future. If it's far enough into the future, the browser may choose to cache the component. This is a good thing, because it saves the browser from having to request that component again from the server for a specified period of time. This speeds up the download because there is one less request to make. You'll look into Expires headers and how to apply them in chapter 4.
- Transfer-Encoding is the type of encoding used to send data back to the browser. In this case it was *chunked*, which means that the data was sent over by the server in a series of chunks instead of all at once.
- The Vary field instructs the proxies to cache two versions of the resource: one compressed and one uncompressed. Without Vary, a server may mistakenly send users the incorrect cached version of an HTML page instead of the correct one for its encoding type.

In chapter 1, you learned that multiple components are downloaded when you request a single URL. These HTTP requests and responses are made for each component in the HTML document and they all have similar fields in the headers. If you refer to the request for www.mozilla.org, you can see that multiple requests are made when you enter the URL. When you request the URL, the HTML document is downloaded, and as the browser parses its contents, it starts to download the additional components it finds inside the HTML.

From the chart in figure 2.3, you can see the multiple GET requests downloaded when you accessed www.mozilla.org. As the browser parsed and located additional components inside the HTML document, it started to download them. Each component is one round-trip that the browser has to make to the server, meaning sending a request and waiting for a response takes time. As a developer, you can find ways to reduce the number of server requests that the browser makes. You can also influence how the browser behaves by telling it to cache the information it downloads. This is what web performance is all about—reducing the number of HTTP requests sent to the server.

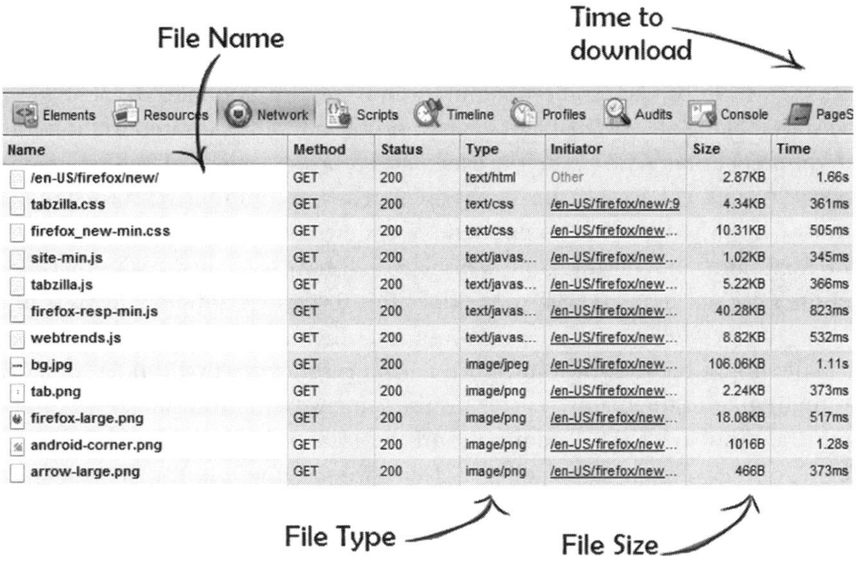
File Name
Time to download
Elements
Resources
Network
Scripts
Timeline
Profiles
Audits
Console
PageS
Name Method Status Type Initiator Size Time
/en-US/firefox/new/ GET 200 text/html Other 2.87KB 1.66s
tabzilla.css GET 200 text/css /en-US/firefox/new/:9 4.34KB 361ms
firefox_new-min.css GET 200 text/css /en-US/firefox/new... 10.31KB 505ms
site-min.js GET 200 text/javas... /en-US/firefox/new... 1.02KB 345ms
tabzilla.js GET 200 text/javas... /en-US/firefox/new... 5.22KB 366ms
firefox-resp-min.js GET 200 text/javas... /en-US/firefox/new... 40.28KB 823ms
webtrends.js GET 200 text/javas... /en-US/firefox/new... 8.82KB 532ms
bg.jpg GET 200 image/jpeg /en-US/firefox/new... 106.06KB 1.11s
tab.png GET 200 image/png /en-US/firefox/new... 2.24KB 373ms
firefox-large.png GET 200 image/png /en-US/firefox/new... 18.08KB 517ms
android-corner.png GET 200 image/png /en-US/firefox/new... 1016B 1.28s
arrow-large.png GET 200 image/png /en-US/firefox/new... 466B 373ms
File Type
File Size

Figure 2.3 Multiple requests to www.mozilla.org

2.1.3 Understanding HTTP status codes

When a request is made to your server for a component on your website, the server returns an HTTP status code, as shown in table 2.1. The status code tells the browser if it retrieved the component and it tells the browser how to react. Status codes can be quite handy when you're debugging an application.

Table 2.1 An HTTP status code list

HTTP status code range	Description
100–1xx	Informational: Request received, continuing process.
200–2xx	Success: The action requested by the client was received, understood, accepted, and processed successfully.
300–3xx	Redirection: The client must take additional action to complete the request.
400–4xx	Client Error: This status code is intended for cases in which the client seems to have made an error.
500–5xx	Server Error: The server failed to fulfill a valid request.

For a full list of status codes, visit http://en.wikipedia.org/wiki/List_of_HTTP_status_codes.

2.2   *Empty cache vs. primed cache*

A web browser stores certain downloaded items for future use in a browser cache folder. Images, JavaScript, CSS, and even entire web pages are examples of cache items. Before you start looking at tools that allow you to profile a website, it's important to understand the differences between an empty cache and a primed cache. The first time you visit a website, you won't have a cache of that site. But as you continue to browse the website, the browser cleverly stores the components you download in this temporary folder cache. The next time you visit the same website, you'll have a primed cache that contains the website's cached items. The browser does this so that on subsequent visits to the same website, it can easily retrieve the components, which speeds up your download time.

The empty cache shown in figure 2.4 represents the first time a user visits a site. Compare that to the primed cache for the same website. You can see the difference in both the number of HTTP requests and the total weight of the web pages. The total weight of the web page on the left is 130K; the total weight for the primed cache on the right is 39.8K. All the components that were saved from the first visit were retrieved from the cache, thus cutting the download time and weight drastically.

An important question to ask yourself when analyzing your website is "How many of my users are first-time visitors (who will have an empty cache) and how many are repeat visitors (who will have a primed cache)?" When you answer this question, based on statistics gathered while using a website analytics package, you'll understand where to focus while you're optimizing your website's performance.

If you don't use a website analytics package or you don't have enough data to determine visitor trends, it can be helpful to think about the domain of your website. Is it an intranet website that might expect a lot of repeat visits throughout the day? Is it a site expecting to attract a lot of new visits? This mindset allows you to put yourself in the shoes of the user so you can improve and enhance their site experience.

It's also important to note that both the primed and empty caches of a browser need to be taken into account when profiling, implementing, and monitoring a web

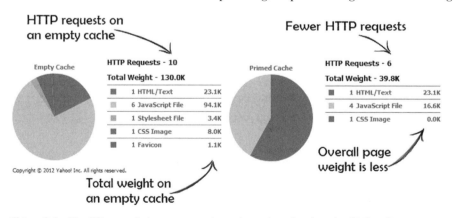

Figure 2.4   The difference between an empty cache and a primed cache. Notice the differences in the total weight and the number of HTTP requests.

page. Sometimes you may find yourself refreshing a web page and getting skewed results because the browser is actually retrieving the components from its cache instead of fetching a fresh version on an empty cache. Most browsers will allow you to refresh a page by hitting the F5 key, which might load the page from cache. But Ctrl-F5 forces a cache refresh, and will guarantee that you'll get the newest content. You may also find that some browsers allow you to force a cache refresh by holding Shift (or Ctrl) and clicking the refresh icon. Keep this in mind when you're profiling your site because you might be profiling a web page that's been updated on the server but isn't reflected in your browser because of caching.

2.3   *Tips and tools for interpreting performance charts*

Now that we've talked about what's going on under the hood when you make a browser request, we can start interpreting performance charts.

To understand how to improve your website's performance, it's vital that you learn how to read performance charts. The most typical charts you'll come across with today's profiling tools are *waterfall charts*, diagrams that show downloads in a linear progression, in a manner that looks like a waterfall.

Most modern browsers come with their own built-in developer tools and a version of a waterfall chart that can be easily accessed via the Tools menu. Most browsers also have a hotkey for developer tools and F12 seems to bring up the developer panel. You may need to check your browser settings first, as different browsers might organize their tools differently. In the next section, you'll go through a brief review of well-known developer tools you can use to produce performance charts; after that, you'll learn how to interpret the data from these charts in greater depth.

2.3.1   *What does it all mean?*

When you look at the waterfall chart in figure 2.5, you can see that it gives you so much more than a series of simple requests.

In a waterfall chart, the length of the bars shows how long a certain resource took to download. In figure 2.5 one bar is extremely long, highlighting an area to investigate. Is the image file size too large? Is the image the correct format? What is causing this image to download so slowly?

The green vertical line (at 1.2) running through all the requests indicates the DOM-ContentLoaded event. The DOMContentLoaded event is triggered when the page's Document Object Model (DOM) is ready, which means that the API for interacting with the content, style, and structure of a page is ready to receive requests from your code.

The blue vertical line (near 3.2) indicates the Load event being fired. The Load event is triggered when the entire page has loaded and is generally the moment when the loading icon in your browser's title bar stops spinning. When this has happened, all JavaScript and Cascading Style Sheets (CSS) have finished loading and have been executed, and all images have been downloaded and displayed. The Load event lines help you see how long it takes for pages to load and helps you understand when the

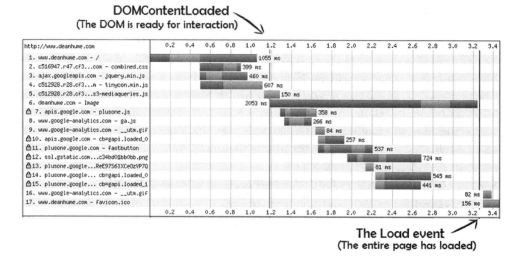

Figure 2.5   Waterfall chart for www.deanhume.com

browser is parsing and loading your website's components. So a green line indicates that the DOMContentLoaded event is triggered and the browser is ready to interact with requests from your code, and a blue line indicates that the Load event has been triggered and all JavaScript and CSS have finished executing. Different developer tools may provide a different color for each vertical line, but they generally mean the same thing.

If you refer to the line in figure 2.5 that was taking a long time to load, you can see that it's pushing the Load event out. There's a gap of whitespace between item 15 being finished loading and item 16 starting. It's as if the image were blocking progress and causing a slight delay, so this is definitely an area to investigate further.

The waterfall chart also shows three JavaScript files being downloaded every time you access the page. Are all three files necessary? Could you reduce these to one request? As you start optimizing your website and looking at ways to improve its performance, you'll need to keep asking yourself these sorts of questions.

Depending on your organization, your website may be image- or style-intensive. Figure 2.6 is the waterfall chart for a popular online clothing store in the UK. You'll see a large number of HTTP requests being made, so many that I had to crop the image.

Due to the nature of the business, high-quality images of the clothes are necessary, but this can have a very negative effect on web page performance. In chapter 7, you'll learn image optimization techniques that reduce the overall size of image files without reducing their quality.

Another area that could be addressed immediately is the number of JavaScript files on the page. Combining them into one file could drastically reduce HTTP requests. In chapter 5, you'll look at minifying and bundling static files, which will reduce the number of HTTP requests and the size of the requests that a browser needs to make.

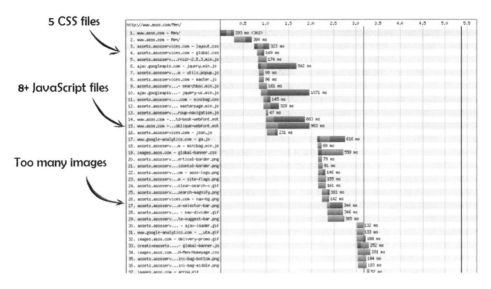

Figure 2.6   Waterfall chart for Asos.com

At first glance, you may notice obvious ways to make performance improvements, but the solution may not be glaringly obvious. If you keep the two main principles (reducing the number of requests and the size of the requests) in mind when profiling your site, finding the solution will be a lot easier.

Each profiling tool will produce waterfall charts with slightly different features. It's up to you to decide which tool and browser you prefer. As you become familiar with your chosen tool, you'll find it easier to read and spot areas for improvement.

2.3.2   Google Chrome developer tools

In figure 2.7, I use Chrome developer tools to show you how to produce a waterfall chart. To access Chrome's developer tools, navigate to the Settings menu and bring up the developer tools in the Tools menu; you could also hit F12.

If you bring up the Network panel and navigate to my website (www.deanhume.com), you can see the components being downloaded as you reach the home page as shown in figure 2.8. The developer tools also show you the waterfall chart and the order in which the components were downloaded.

The waterfall chart also takes latency into account. *Latency* is the amount of time it takes to open a connection to the server and is associated with the round-trip time that it takes for a request to reach the server and return to the user. The amount of latency depends largely on how far away the user is from the server. It's shown in the lighter shade within each bar.

The chart is color coded, with each hue representing a content type, such as JavaScript files, CSS, or images. This helps you see and visually group the different content types.

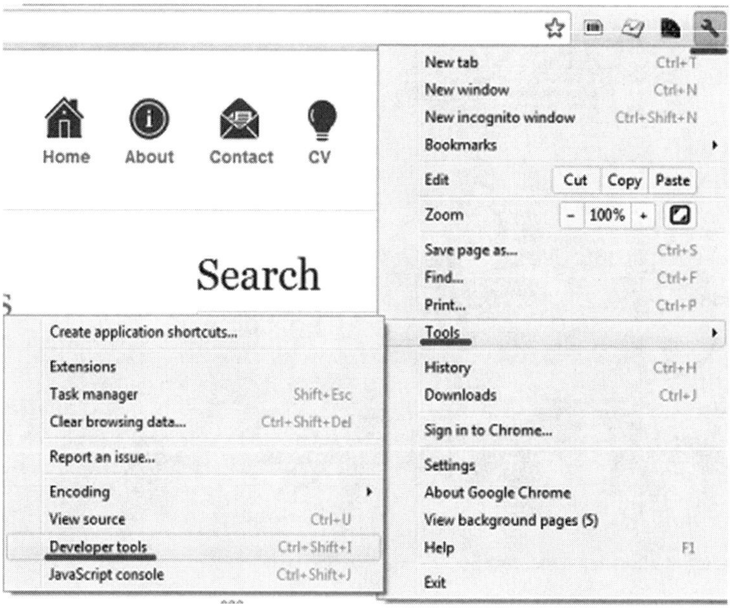

Figure 2.7   Accessing Chrome developer tools

The Chrome developer tools also allow you to edit HTML and CSS on the fly, which is a handy way to develop quickly and make small changes without having to reload the page. Next, you'll run through a few other browser developer tools and show the differences between waterfall charts and other profiling tools.

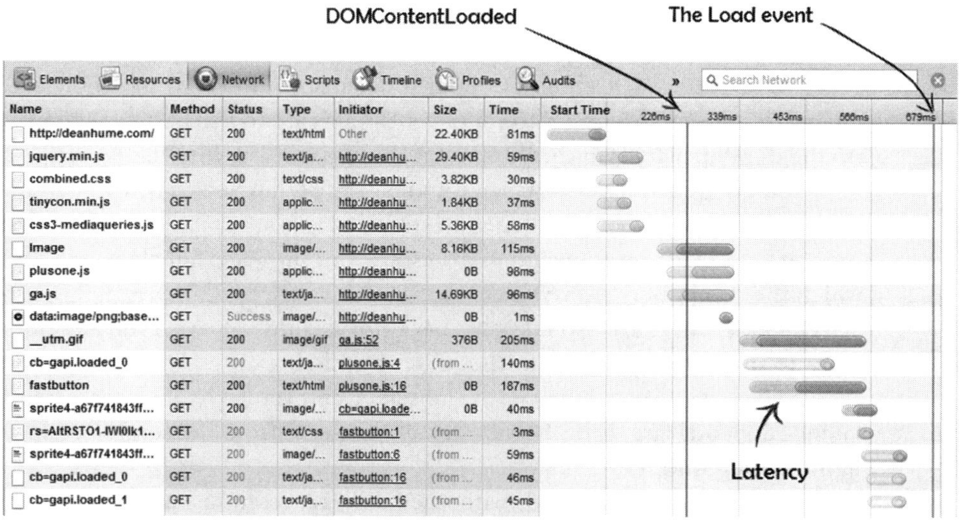

Figure 2.8   Waterfall chart for www.deanhume.com using Chrome developer tools. The figure also shows the latency that can sometimes be associated with the download time of a component.

NOTE Remember that certain components on a web page may be cached, which can affect your waterfall chart's accuracy. Run the tool and produce charts for both primed and empty caches in order to get a more complete picture.

2.3.3 *Internet Explorer developer tools*

The developer tools in Internet Explorer have been around since IE 6 and have evolved with each new version. In IE 9, the tools allow you to debug JavaScript, HTML, and CSS as well as profile the performance of a web page using the handy profiling reports. They can be easily accessed by hitting the F12 key, as seen in figure 2.9.

2.3.4 *Firebug*

Firebug is a free and open source tool that was originally built as an extension for Firefox. It has been around since 2006 and is a solid and proven tool. Firebug was one of the first developer tools to produce a waterfall chart, and most other developer tools have produced similar waterfall charts based on this original style. Much like Chrome's developer tools, it allows you to edit HTML and CSS on the fly.

Using the Net tab allows you to easily view a waterfall chart, and by expanding on the individual nodes, you can view the HTTP requests and responses. Although Firebug was originally intended for Firefox, it's also available as a plugin for Chrome. For more information, visit getfirebug.com.

2.3.5 *Safari Web Inspector*

If you develop for Mac users or just prefer to use Safari, it also has a free tool, called Web Inspector, which allows you to inspect network traffic. You may also notice that the layout and design are very similar to the Chrome developer tools. Safari and Chrome are powered by WebKit.

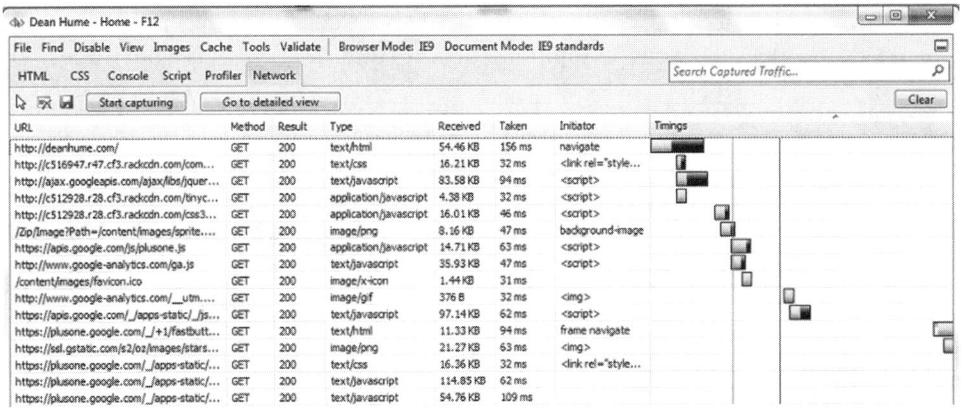

Figure 2.9 Waterfall chart for www.deanhume.com using IE developer tools

2.3.6   *HTTPWatch*

HTTPWatch is an integrated HTTP sniffer for IE and Firefox that allows you to watch and "sniff" the HTTP traffic coming to and from your website. It provides a great set of tools that allow you to easily profile your site's performance, as well. It doesn't come built into any browsers, but a free basic version and an advanced version with more features can be purchased and downloaded from www.httpwatch.com.

2.3.7   *WebPagetest*

You can find an extremely handy tool to profile your site at www.webpagetest.org. It isn't built into any browser, but it can provide a wealth of information about any website (figure 2.10). Simply visit the site and enter the URL you wish to profile.

WebPagetest is an open source project that's developed and supported primarily by Google. Many partners also work with WebPagetest and provide a test location for you to run your site against. I really like the way you can profile your site against a location from almost anywhere in the world, using multiple browsers. It's especially handy if you need to see what your users would see if they accessed your site from halfway across the world. These test locations provide useful insight into the round-trips the browser will make to download the required components. There is even an option to record video of the page as it loads, which can be very useful to compare and review page rendering.

WebPagetest provides a breakdown of the first view and the repeat view, allowing you to see how many requests you saved by using caching, Expires headers, and so on. You can also experiment with different advanced features if your website has a complex setup. Throughout this book, I will refer to www.webpagetest.org because it provides a great set of charts that give us an in-depth look at a website's performance.

2.3.8   *Fiddler*

Another fantastic free tool is Fiddler. This web debugging proxy logs all network traffic between your computer and the internet and lets you inspect traffic, set

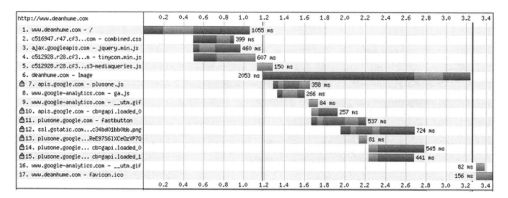

Figure 2.10   Waterfall chart for www.deanhume.com using www.webpagetest.org

breakpoints, and "fiddle" with incoming or outgoing data. It can be quite interesting to fire up Fiddler and watch the requests coming and going from your PC, let alone the website that you are profiling!

The Fiddler dashboard gives you an in-depth look at the HTTP requests and allows you to create and test HTTP requests yourself. Fiddler also offers a whole host of other great features. For more information, point your browser at www.fiddler2.com/fiddler2.

2.4 Performance rules to live by

In 2007, Steve Souders, at the time Chief Performance Yahoo! at Yahoo!, created a set of 14 rules for faster front-end performance. These rules, shown in table 2.2, are outlined in his book, *High Performance Web Sites*, and every single one is widely accepted as best practice in web performance today.

Table 2.2   Steve Souders's rules for faster front-end performance

Rule Number	Description
1	Make fewer HTTP requests
2	Use a content delivery network
3	Add an Expires header
4	Compress components with Gzip
5	Put CSS at the top
6	Move JavaScript to the bottom
7	Avoid CSS expressions
8	Make JavaScript and CSS external
9	Reduce DNS lookups
10	Minify JavaScript
11	Avoid redirects
12	Remove duplicate scripts
13	Turn off ETags
14	Make AJAX cacheable and small

As the web has evolved, the number of rules has increased, but every core concept in this book is based on Souders's 14 rules. There may be newer browsers that can handle HTML5, but these original rules have been proven and tested, and they underpin everything that you are trying to achieve.

Many of these rules closely align with this book's table of contents. As you progress through the chapters, you'll learn about the performance rules, as well as some of the newer concepts that have evolved with the introduction of HTML5 and advances in JavaScript.

There are a lot of performance techniques and methods that can be applied to your website and trying to remember them all when you're profiling your site can be quite daunting. This is where a performance-profiling tool can be very helpful. Instead of remembering each and every technique, these tools take the hard work out of profiling and provide a set of suggestions and best practices that can be applied to your website. Let's look at two such performance-analysis tools, Yahoo! YSlow and Google PageSpeed.

2.4.1   Yahoo! YSlow

YSlow is a great add-on for many browsers and it offers suggestions for improving a web page's performance. It's free and can be downloaded from http://developer .yahoo.com/yslow/ for Firefox, Chrome, Opera, and Safari. The tool runs against a set of 23 rules that affect web page performance. Throughout the remainder of this book, you'll come back to this tool to see how each improvement you make boosts your performance score.

YSlow provides a grade and overall performance score for your URL. It grades A as high performance and F as poor. You should, obviously, always aim for the highest grade you can obtain because each step closer to an A improves your web page performance. Figure 2.11 shows performance areas on my website that need to be improved.

In figure 2.11 you'll notice that the overall performance score for my website is quite high, but one area scored an E. Obviously I need to add an Expires header to

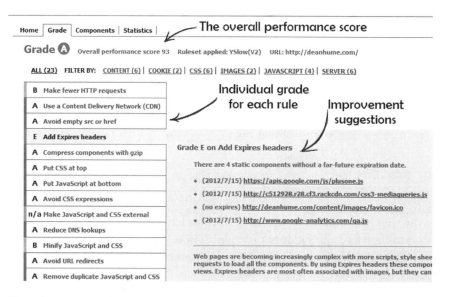

Figure 2.11   Yahoo! YSlow tool run against www.deanhume.com

certain components on the web page. As you recall from examples earlier in the chapter, these Expires headers let the browser know that the component doesn't need to be downloaded again because the content hasn't changed. It will only expire in the future—this saves the browser a round-trip to the server again, thus speeding up the load time. You'll look at code and the different ways in which you can add Expires headers to the components in your web page in chapter 4.

2.4.2 Google PageSpeed

Google also has a handy performance tool called PageSpeed, shown in figure 2.12, which can be added to both Firefox and Chrome. It's very similar to YSlow and was built using the same performance rules set out by the Yahoo! performance team. PageSpeed has grown to become a great tool that allows you to easily profile your site. If you would like to try the tool before adding it to your browser, Google offers you the ability to do so on the PageSpeed Insights web page (https://developers.google.com/speed/pagespeed/insights).

In figure 2.12, you can see the results of a test run against my site. Much like YSlow, it has given me a similar suggestion, letting me know that I need to use browser caching by setting an expiration date on some resources. The PageSpeed tool provides a very simple interface that suggests only the improvements you need to make. Unlike YSlow, it doesn't give you a breakdown of the components or the empty versus primed cache view. I find it very helpful to have the full dashboard that YSlow provides, but I also like to incorporate the performance results from Google PageSpeed into my overall performance profiling. Each tool provides its own rule set and logic to determine the score.

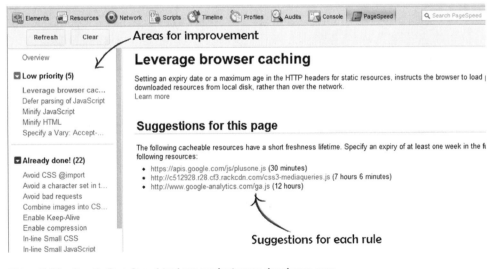

Figure 2.12   Google PageSpeed tool run against www.deanhume.com

NOTE Some of the performance profiling tools may offer a setting that enables you to autorun the tests every time a web page is loaded. Although this may be helpful during testing and development, remember that it needs to process a full set of rules and code, which may take time. It may feel as if a web page is running slowly, but actually it's the profiling tool running in the background. Don't forget to turn it off when you aren't using it!

2.5   Summary

In this chapter, you started off learning the basics of HTTP and understanding how the browser makes a request to the server and gets a response. Next, you had a brief summary of the tools that are freely available with most browsers. These developer tools will help you start profiling and analyzing HTTP requests and responses from your websites. The waterfall chart is the most widely used when it comes to profiling your site and it displays the component downloads over a timeline. You evaluated two different web pages with a waterfall chart and saw how you could reduce the overall number of HTTP requests. You also became familiar with two tools that help you measure your applications' performance, as well as suggest areas for improvement. You'll use these tools throughout the book as you work to improve the sample application's speed.

Now that you have a good grasp of the basics of web performance, it's time to start improving your website. In the next chapter you'll learn how to apply compression to your website and make significant speed gains.

Part 2

General performance best practices

Part 1 helped you understand the inner workings of web pages and the life-cycle of a web page request. This knowledge is vital to effectively improve the performance of your web pages and it will help guide you through part 2. You are about to start applying performance techniques that will improve and enhance the speed of your web pages.

In these seven chapters you will become familiar with the sample application used throughout this book. As you progress and apply the performance-enhancing techniques to the Surf Store application, you will notice a decrease in its page load times, and a reduction in the overall page weight of each page. Each technique is a building block that will make your pages lighter and load times quicker.

IIS plays a big role in this part of the book, and you begin by looking at compression and the benefits that it brings to web page performance. HTTP caching is another important best practice that you can use to leverage the caching capabilities of your user's browser. You will learn how to apply both of these techniques using IIS and ASP.NET.

In addition, you will look at the new bundling and minification features in ASP.NET 4.5 and how you can use them to drastically reduce the weight of your JavaScript and CSS files. Both file types play an important role on the web today and understanding where and how to position them within your HTML will squeeze the best load times out of the browser. In this part, you'll learn techniques that can be applied by using HTML5 to improve the performance of your web pages.

Images on a web page are frequently the big, ugly brother of web page performance; they are heavy and often neglected. You will learn how to use image optimization tools that will reduce the size of these images and how you can make image optimization a regular feature of your websites.

Finally, you'll learn about Content Delivery Networks (CDNs) and how you can harness the power of these geographically distributed servers to serve faster web pages to your users throughout the world.

Compression 3

This chapter covers

- The pros and cons of compression
- The types of compression available
- The sample application used in this book
- How to apply compression to a website

In this chapter we'll look at the impact compression can have on your site—optimizing front-end performance and taking you closer to your goal of a grade A performance website.

By using compression, you'll reduce the size of each HTTP request a web page makes, and each reduction will lighten, as it were, the overall weight of the page. By the end of the chapter, you'll be able to optimize your website with a number of compression techniques in the .NET web technology stack. We'll go through examples that are applicable to IIS, ASP.NET MVC, and Web Forms.

3.1 What is compression?

Compression is an algorithm that eliminates unwanted redundancy from a file in order to create one that is smaller than the original representation. If both the server and the browser understand this algorithm, it can be applied to the response

The browser indicates that it supports compression.

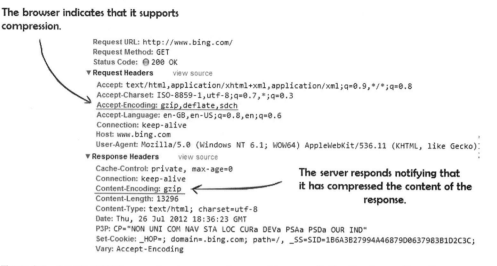

The server responds notifying that it has compressed the content of the response.

Figure 3.1   A typical HTTP request and response for www.bing.com. Notice the Accept-Encoding and Content-Encoding headers.

and request. Web browsers indicate that they support compression in the headers that are sent to the server in the HTTP request. The web server sees this header in the request and will try to compress the response that it sends back.

Compression is extremely easy to implement and is a quick win. You're about to get up and running using compression, but first it's important to understand the types of compression.

Look at the HTTP request in figure 3.1 and you'll notice that the browser sent the server a header called Accept-Encoding. This header notifies the server that it supports compression as well as the types of compression it supports, in this case, Gzip, Deflate, and SDCH. Depending on the type of compression your browser supports, the server will then compress its content accordingly and return a header in the HTTP response called Content-Encoding. In the case of figure 3.1, the server has returned a response notifying the browser that it compressed the data in Gzip format.

3.2   *Why should I use compression?*

In order to test the effectiveness of compression and evaluate the savings it could have on different file types, I took a few common files that you'll encounter and compressed them using Gzip. The results are shown in table 3.1.

Table 3.1   Gzip compression's effect on file sizes

File type	File size without compression	File size after compression with Gzip	Savings
HTML	6.52 KB	2.43 KB	62.74%
CSS	91.57 KB	21.12 KB	76.93%

Table 3.1   Gzip compression's effect on file sizes *(continued)*

File type	File size without compression	File size after compression with Gzip	Savings
CSS	13.51 KB	3.89 KB	71.21%
JavaScript	1.75 KB	1.18 KB	32.58%
Image	6.76 KB	6.51 KB	3.7%

In two of the files, there is a massive difference, with savings of over 70%. Gzip compression works by finding similar strings within a text file, and replacing those strings temporarily to make the overall file size smaller. This form of compression is particularly well suited for the web because HTML and CSS files usually contain plenty of repeated strings, such as whitespace, tags, and style definitions. You'll notice that the biggest savings were made on text-based files and there were hardly any gains on the image file. Image files are already compressed, so applying compression to them doesn't bring much reward.

There is also a direct correlation between the size of the file and the amount of savings (compression) that takes place. As a general rule the larger the file the greater the savings, primarily because larger files contain more whitespace and character repetition.

Chrome Developer tools allow you to compare file sizes before and after applying compression. Figure 3.2 shows these differences.

> **NOTE**   In chapter 2 you used a variety of developer tools. By hitting the F12 key on most computers, you can easily bring up the developer tools in your browser of choice.

Twitter Bootstrap is a popular CSS framework that will help you develop your CSS styles quickly so you can get your project running in no time. The CSS files contain a lot of whitespace and style tags, which make them perfect for compression. On the main bootstrap.css file the file size was cut down to 21.12 KB, saving almost 76% on the file size! This is a perfect example of why you should compress your CSS and JavaScript files.

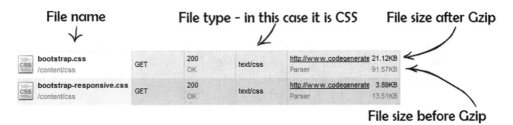

Figure 3.2   The difference in file sizes before and after using Gzip

3.3   *Pros and cons of compression*

When first working with compression, some web developers will compress only the HTML file they're sending to the browser. They don't compress all the other components that make up a web page, such as the CSS, JavaScript, XML, and JSON files. It's far better to compress as many components as you can, whenever you can, to reduce the total page weight as much as possible.

There is also a cost associated with compression; the server needs to apply an algorithm to compress the files, and this can affect the CPU usage on the server. There is a bit of a tradeoff between CPU usage and the savings in file size, but if the compression settings are controlled and fine-tuned, the benefit of compressing files can far outweigh the extra CPU usage on the server.

As a general rule, it's best to compress files that are larger than 1–2 KB. Even if the server manages to compress the file by 50%, you'll save only 1 KB. Every byte counts on a web page, but the server still needs to work hard to process each file, regardless of its size. By asking the server to compress files this small, you're placing an unnecessary load on the server, which could have a detrimental effect on server response time.

You should also make sure that you don't try to compress PDF, zip, and image files, because these types of files have already been highly compressed. Processing them again on the server only adds an unnecessary load on the CPU that won't reap any rewards and can affect the client wait time. Fortunately, IIS 7+ offers a great feature that throttles CPU usage.

Throttling CPU usage means that when CPU usage gets beyond a certain level, IIS will automatically stop compressing pages. When usage drops to an acceptable level, the CPU will start compressing pages again. This feature is a great safety net because it ensures that your application won't be affected if it does come under heavy load.

IIS trades bandwidth and page load times for server CPU usage. So when the load is high enough that IIS starts throttling the CPU, the site reverts to its precompression performance levels, sacrificing the benefits of compression in order to keep the application running. You'll learn about this in more detail later in the chapter.

3.4   *Types of compression*

Compression capability has been built into web servers and web clients to make better use of available bandwidth and to provide faster transmission speeds between both. There are many types of compression, but almost all of them have little browser support. When you're looking at all the options, it's important not to become too worried because ultimately IIS will take care of compression for you. You'll look at the most common compression options now, which are the ones you'll most likely encounter in your day-to-day life as a developer.

3.4.1   *Gzip*

Gzip is a lossless data compression algorithm that compresses files and data without affecting the integrity of its contents. It allows the original data to be reconstructed from the compressed data. When compared to other types of compression commonly used in HTTP traffic, Gzip is known to achieve higher compression ratios, resulting in smaller file sizes. To date, it's also the most widely used format because it's available freely and isn't blocked by any patents or other restrictions. Because this is the most common compression method and almost every browser that you'll encounter today supports it, this is the compression format you'll focus on in this chapter.

3.4.2 Deflate

Another type of compression you might see browsers using in the Accept-Encoding request headers is Deflate. Much like Gzip, Deflate is a lossless data compression algorithm that compresses files and data without affecting the overall integrity of its contents. There isn't a lot of browser support for this type of compression, so it isn't as widely used. You'll often see that browsers that support Deflate will also support Gzip, but because Gzip achieves a higher compression ratio and smaller file sizes, the latter is often the preferred compression method. Fortunately for IIS users, IIS 7+ supports Deflate. This widens the variety of compression methods that you're able to serve your users.

3.4.3 SDCH

A newer type of compression that has recently started to appear in the Google Chrome Browser is SDCH (Shared Dictionary Compression over HTTP). Google has proposed it as a modification to HTTP 1.1. The support for it is minimal; however, it's still worth mentioning because it's a new type of compression that could become more widespread in the future.

3.5 Accept-Encoding

Let's look at a typical HTTP response before it's decompressed by the browser. Figure 3.3 shows an HTTP response from msdn.microsoft.com.

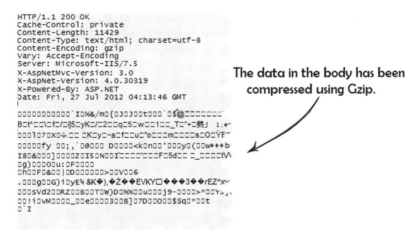

Figure 3.3 An HTTP Response for msdn.microsoft.com. The image is cropped because of its size, but note the encoded text in the response body.

As you can see, the content is encoded and is garbled. This is what the browser sees before it's decompressed and displayed on the screen.

What happens when an error occurs on the server? What happens if the browser doesn't support the compression type even if the server sends it back? Mistakes can happen and the user might see a garbled response on their screen like the data in figure 3.3. This rarely happens, but it's important to have a fallback plan for such instances. This is where the Vary header comes in.

The Vary header allows the server to return different cached versions of the page depending on whether or not the browser requested Gzip encoding. The Vary header instructs the cache to store a different version of the page if there's any variation in the indicated header. I like to think of the Vary header as fail-safe because it instructs the server to vary its cache based on the Content-Encoding type. The server then creates a separate cached copy of the page for each Content-Encoding type, which means that each Content-Encoding type requested by the browser will have a specific cached version ready for it.

3.6   *The Surf Store application*

To help you apply what you're learning in this book, you'll create a sample application called Surf Store in this chapter and build upon it throughout the remainder of the book. You'll be able to apply each technique you learn and run through the performance cycle that we discussed in chapter 1. The Surf Store application simulates an e-commerce store and will be similar to many sites you see online today. The sample application may seem rather basic, but its web pages contain all the elements that a standard website would have.

The Surf Store application shown in figure 3.4 contains three main pages: a Home page, an About page, and a Contact page. The Home page lists the products that are for sale and the product categories. On the left side of the Home page, you'll notice

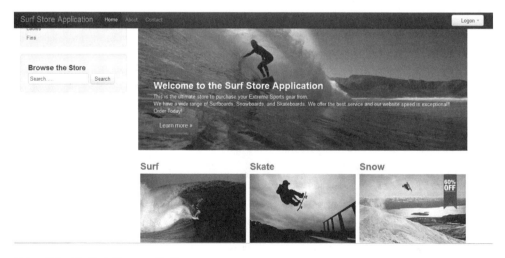

Figure 3.4   The Surf Store application

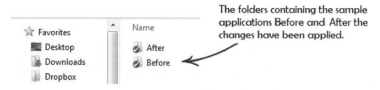

Figure 3.5   The Surf Store's download folder structure

that top-level categories are represented by links in a menu. These links, as well as the images on the page, allow you to navigate to a Product page that lists the products in that particular category. The About page contains a short description of the website, and the Contact page contains a form that allows website users to contact the Surf Store staff. Each page contains JavaScript, CSS, HTML, and images, and all of these are the front-end elements that we're trying to improve upon.

You'll have the choice of building the sample application in either ASP.NET Web Forms or ASP.NET MVC. Then you'll be able to use whichever part of the ASP.NET development framework you're most comfortable with. In order to use the Surf Store application, you'll need a copy of Visual Studio 2012 or a free copy of Visual Studio Express 2012, which is available for download at www.microsoft.com/visualstudio/11/en-us/products/express. I've made the project source code available for download on Github at https://github.com/deanhume/FastASPNetWebsites. Once you've navigated to the source code on Github, you can download all the files you need as a single zip file.

As you progress through the book, you'll apply the different optimization techniques you'll learn about in each chapter and compare the pre- and post-optimization results. Once you've downloaded the code, most chapters in the book will have a corresponding folder that contains Before and After subfolders, as shown in figure 3.5. You'll be able to use the concepts described in each chapter and apply them to the code in the Before folder. If you're unsure or become stuck, refer to the completed code in the After folder. Once you've reached chapter 12, you'll notice a dramatically different site that is very fast!

3.7   *Adding compression to your website*

Adding compression to your website is extremely easy and rewarding. Your hosting solution will determine which techniques to use. If you have full control of your server and are able to log into the IIS settings, it's advisable to apply the changes to the IIS settings first.

There are two different types of content that get compressed on the server: static and dynamic. Static content typically is associated with file types that don't change often:

- HTML, HTM files
- JS, CSS
- TXT
- DOC (Word)

- XLS (Excel)
- PPT (PowerPoint)

Once IIS has compressed static content, it caches it, which increases compression performance. Once the static files have been compressed, IIS 7 serves any further requests from the compressed copy in the cache directory.

Dynamic content typically is associated with file types that change often and can be produced by server-side code. Examples include JSON, XML, and ASPX. Dynamic content is processed the same way as static content; the only difference is that once it's been processed, it isn't cached to disk. Due to the nature of the files and because they could change on every request, IIS processes and compresses them each time they're requested.

3.7.1   *Using IIS to add compression to a website*

Now we're going to run through an example, applying compression to the Surf Store application in no time with IIS. You may not always have direct access to IIS, but using IIS is the easiest and quickest way to add compression to your site. If you've never before set up a website using IIS and would like to learn how to use your local machine as a web development server, please refer to the appendix of this book.

To start adding compression to your website, navigate to the Internet Information Services (IIS) Manager (figure 3.6).

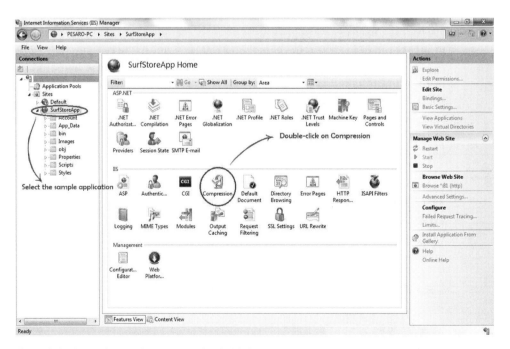

Figure 3.6   Step 1 in enabling compression in IIS 7

If you're using Windows Server 2008 or Windows Server 2008 R2:

- On the taskbar, click Start, point to Administrative Tools, then click Internet Information Services (IIS) Manager.

If you're using Windows Vista or Windows 7:

- On the taskbar, click Start, then click Control Panel.
- Double-click Administrative Tools, then double-click Internet Information Services (IIS) Manager.

Next, check the boxes to enable dynamic and static compression and click Apply (figure 3.7).

It's as simple as that! If you view the same website using your browser, you can immediately see the differences. If a client is not capable of HTTP compression, it will not pass that header and IIS 7 will always return uncompressed content. Figure 3.8 illustrates how the requested file sizes have undergone huge reductions. The largest JavaScript file (the jQuery library) went from 246.95 KB to 95.71 KB, reducing the total file size by 151.24 KB, a 61.25% savings. The CSS file that's being used as this application's base (Twitter Bootstrap) went from 97.55 KB to 21.97 KB, which works out to a 77.5% reduction of the total file size. That's a pretty impressive saving.

As you can see, the individual file sizes have been reduced, but how has this affected the overall page weight? It went from 985.55 KB to 745.29 KB, which is almost a 25% reduction in total page weight! To enable compression on the server, all you needed to do was check two check boxes, a simple act that shaved about 240 KB off the total weight of the page.

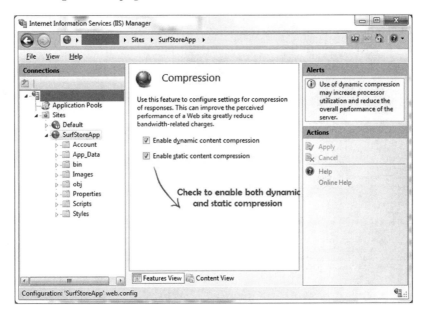

Figure 3.7   Step 2 in enabling compression in IIS 7

The HTML size is reduced.

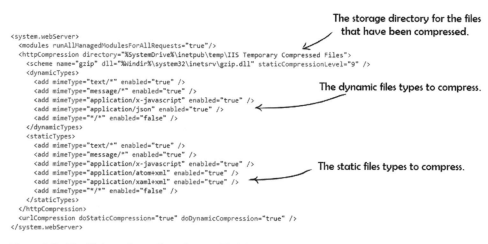

Name Path	Method	Status Text	Type	Initiator	Size Content	Time Latency
/SurfStoreApp/ /SurfStoreApp	GET	200 OK	text/html	Other	1.98KB 6.10KB	175ms 175ms
bootstrap.css /SurfStoreApp/Styles	GET	200 OK	text/css	/SurfStoreApp/:10 Parser	21.97KB 97.50KB	124ms 124ms
bootstrap-responsive /SurfStoreApp/Styles	GET	200 OK	text/css	/SurfStoreApp/:11 Parser	4.07KB 14.11KB	46ms 40ms
jquery-1.7.2.js /SurfStoreApp/Scripts	GET	200 OK	application/...	/SurfStoreApp/:11 Parser	95.71KB 246.95KB	157ms 156ms
bootstrap-alert.js /SurfStoreApp/Scripts	GET	200 OK	application/...	/SurfStoreApp/:11 Parser	1.56KB 2.34KB	30ms 30ms

JavaScript and CSS have been reduced.

Figure 3.8   The file size savings after adding Gzip to the Surf Store application

3.7.2   *Using a Web.config file to add compression to a website*

Okay, so what happens when you don't have access to the server? You may be using shared hosting to host your website, or you may be working in an environment where you don't have access to IIS Manager. Fortunately, you can still configure and enable compression for your website by using the Web.config file. If you aren't already familiar with Web.config, it's a standard XML file that's included whenever you start building a new ASP.NET application. It contains all the configuration settings for the application and it allows you to control and fine-tune your application's compression settings. Figure 3.9 shows the code you'll need to add to your Web.config file in order to enable compression on the server.

You can specify the different file or MIME types that you want the server to compress under the `dynamicTypes` and `staticTypes` elements in the Web.config file. Both

The storage directory for the files that have been compressed.

```
<system.webServer>
  <modules runAllManagedModulesForAllRequests="true"/>
  <httpCompression directory="%SystemDrive%\inetpub\temp\IIS Temporary Compressed Files">
    <scheme name="gzip" dll="%Windir%\system32\inetsrv\gzip.dll" staticCompressionLevel="9" />
    <dynamicTypes>
      <add mimeType="text/*" enabled="true" />
      <add mimeType="message/*" enabled="true" />
      <add mimeType="application/x-javascript" enabled="true" />
      <add mimeType="application/json" enabled="true" />
      <add mimeType="*/*" enabled="false" />
    </dynamicTypes>
    <staticTypes>
      <add mimeType="text/*" enabled="true" />
      <add mimeType="message/*" enabled="true" />
      <add mimeType="application/x-javascript" enabled="true" />
      <add mimeType="application/atom+xml" enabled="true" />
      <add mimeType="application/xaml+xml" enabled="true" />
      <add mimeType="*/*" enabled="false" />
    </staticTypes>
  </httpCompression>
  <urlCompression doStaticCompression="true" doDynamicCompression="true" />
</system.webServer>
```

The dynamic files types to compress.

The static files types to compress.

Figure 3.9   The Web.config settings that enable IIS compression

elements are visible in figure 3.9. It isn't advisable to process everything. As you'll recall, some file types are already compressed so you'll only waste valuable CPU resources if you attempt to compress them again. Remember that images and PDFs are already quite compressed, so the savings you'll gain from compressing these file types will be minimal. The most common file types that should be compressed are:

- CSS
- JavaScript
- JSON
- RSS
- HTML
- XML

The `urlCompression` element is another quick way to enable or disable compression on your website. The `urlCompression` element is shown in figure 3.9.

It only has three attributes: `doStaticCompression`, `doDynamicCompression`, and `dynamicCompressionBeforeCache`. The first two settings are simple on/off switches; the third attribute specifies whether IIS will dynamically compress content that has not been cached. When the `dynamicCompressionBeforeCache` attribute is enabled, IIS will dynamically compress the content the first time a request is made. Every request will be compressed dynamically until the response has been added to the cache directory. Once the compressed response is added to the cache directory, the cached response is sent to clients for subsequent requests.

Another compression setting that I find useful is `minFileSizeForComp`, which stands for "minimum file size for compression." Earlier in the chapter, we talked about how compression works best on larger files and how CPU levels are affected when it has to process a lot of smaller files. Using the `minFileSizeForComp` attribute allows you to set a minimum number of bytes a file must contain in order to use on-demand compression. The default size that it will compress in IIS 7.5 is 2,700 bytes and in IIS 7 it is 256 bytes.

Earlier in the chapter, I mentioned that IIS has the ability to throttle the CPU usage of the server. It gives you the ability to specify the percentage of CPU utilization at which dynamic compression will be disabled or re-enabled. You can specify the CPU percentage at which dynamic compression will be disabled by adding and setting the optional `DynamicCompressionDisableCpuUsage` attribute in your Web.config file. The attribute is set with an integer field and represents the percentage at which it will disable itself. On the opposite side, the `DynamicCompressionEnableCpuUsage` attribute specifies the percentage of CPU utilization at which dynamic compression will be re-enabled. These two attributes are useful when you have to keep CPU usage on your server to a minimum.

There are many other great attributes you can use to fine-tune your compression settings. For more information and the full list, please visit www.iis.NET/ConfigReference/system.webServer/httpCompression.

3.7.3 *Adding compression with other techniques*

There are other ways to add compression to your website in ASP.NET, but I wouldn't recommend them. Applying compression to your application with IIS and Web.config is the simplest and most effective way of optimizing your website. They both integrate with IIS and their settings can be maintained easily. If you're interested in other compression methods, there are a few NuGet packages, custom-written libraries, and techniques you can use to add compression to your website programmatically, but as a general rule, I try to stay clear of them. Writing code to add compression to your site can cause unwanted side effects and if there's an error, your users could be presented with a garbled page. Often you'll find that adding the compression programmatically will end up compressing only the HTML, but we want to compress as many components in the web page as possible. It's best to leave this up to the built-in server tools and let them handle the delicate details for you.

Another downside to using other compression techniques is that you can't control CPU usage or fine-tune processes the way you can with the Web.config method. With all that said, you may find yourself in a situation where you can't use the native IIS settings or your Web.config file. Proceed with caution!

3.8 *The results*

You've just applied compression to the Surf Store application using either IIS or Web.config. Now you can use some of the tools that were discussed in chapter 2 to monitor the results of the changes you've made. Before applying any compression to the Surf Store application, you should use the Google PageSpeed extension to generate a list of suggestions and best practices. Figure 3.10 shows that compression is at the top of the list, and that the PageSpeed score is low.

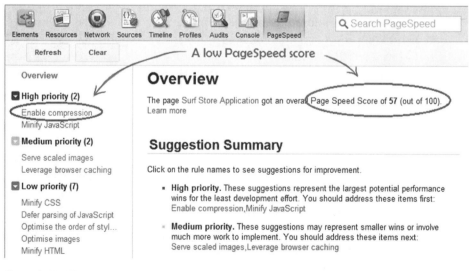

Figure 3.10 The performance score of the Surf Store application before adding compression. The Google PageSpeed tool was used to determine the score.

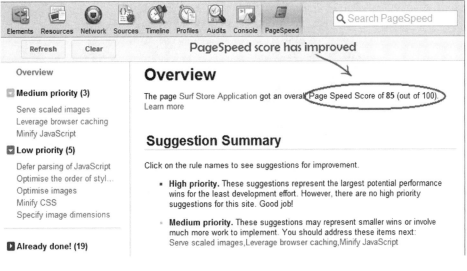

Figure 3.11   The Surf Store application's performance score, after compression, as calculated by the Google PageSpeed tool

Now that you've optimized the Surf Store application, you should run the PageSpeed tool to see how much the site's speed was improved. You can see the results in figure 3.11. After adding compression, the site jumped from a 57 PageSpeed score to an 85. You also managed to cut the total page weight down from 985.55 KB to 745.29 KB. That's a healthy reduction of 240.26 KB!

I suggest you run the Yahoo! YSlow tool on the same version of the site as a comparison. YSlow yielded similar results, as you can see in figure 3.12. The Yahoo! YSlow score jumped from a C to a B grade, and the score for adding compression jumped to an A.

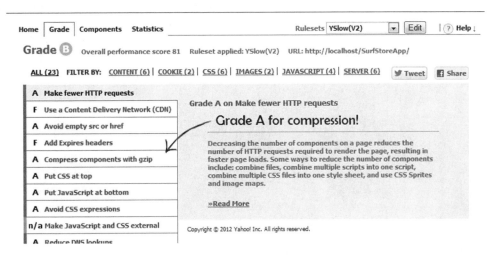

Figure 3.12   The Surf Store application's performance score as calculated by the Yahoo! YSlow tool

Average Bytes per Page by Content Type

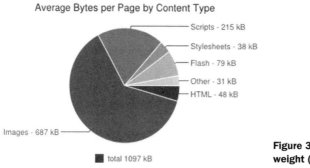

Figure 3.13   The average total page weight (source: HttpArchive.org)

You may be wondering why the total page weight originally came in at 985.55 KB and why the total weight is such a high number, even after compression.

Figure 3.13, a repeat of figure 1.3, shows us that, on average, the total weight for a web page is around 1.09 MB. The Surf Store application is intended to be as close to that number as possible, so you can simulate real-world examples when you run through these exercises.

3.9   *Summary*

In 2009, a Google blog[1] claimed that more than 99 human years are wasted every day because of uncompressed content. Such content wastes bandwidth and increases the amount of time users spend waiting for a web page to load. Although support for compression is a standard feature of all modern browsers, there are still many instances when users don't receive compressed content.

In this chapter you learned some simple techniques to enable compression on your website. Simply updating IIS or updating your application's Web.config settings applied compression to the Surf Store application. There was also a marked improvement in the reduction of the total page weight and the performance tools' scores.

By adding compression, you're moving one step closer to a speedy, optimized website. As you can see from the examples in this chapter, it takes almost no time to implement compression on your website. If you only add one performance feature to your website, I highly recommend that you add compression today.

---

[1]   Arvind Jain and Jason Glasgow, "Use Compression to Make the Web Faster," Google Developers Blog, June 2013, http://mng.bz/e6bp.

Caching: The sell-by date

It's important to know where the bulk of your website visits come from. If you have a lot of repeat visits or if many people view more than one page before leaving your website, then HTTP caching can have a positive effect on your page load times. Modern browsers are really clever; they can interpret and understand a variety of HTTP requests and responses and are capable of storing and caching data until it's needed. With the introduction of HTML5 and CSS3, modern browsers have become capable of achieving so much more than they could a few years ago. I like to think of the browser's ability to cache information as the sell-by date on milk. In the same way that you might keep milk in your fridge until it reaches its expiration date before replacing it with a new carton of milk, browsers can cache information about a website for a set duration of time. After

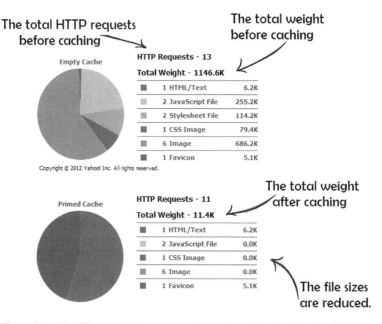

Figure 4.1 The difference between an empty cache and a primed cache. Notice the difference in their total weights.

the data has expired, it will simply go and fetch the updated version upon your next visit to the website.

We briefly covered the differences between a primed cache and an empty cache in chapter 2. When you visit a website for the first time, your browser stores the components you download in a temporary cache. It does this so it can easily retrieve the components the next time you visit the same website. This, in turn, speeds up your download time.

The chart at the top of figure 4.1 shows the components of a web page that have not yet been cached. The total page weight is quite high and the browser will need to make 13 HTTP requests to fully load all the components it needs when a user visits the website for the first time. The chart at the bottom of the figure shows a primed cache for a user who has already visited the website with HTTP caching enabled. The total page weight is down to 11.4K from 1146.6K and most of the HTTP requests that it needs to make all came from within the browser's own cache.

HTTP caching's main purpose is to use the browser's cache to its advantage. If a user revisits a website, their browser can simply retrieve the components it needs from the browser cache instead of hitting the server again.

4.1 What is HTTP caching?

Most websites today are made up of similar components. Often these components, such as CSS and JavaScript, are shared across multiple pages, so by caching them, you effectively speed up any other pages on your site that a first time visitor would see as he browses your website.

Although the majority of visitors to your website might be new, remember that a large percentage of them might be returning. These returnees will experience extremely fast load times and benefit greatly from HTTP caching. Depending on the nature of your website, you may experience high volumes of returning visitors or really low numbers of returning visitors. Whichever way you look at it, adding HTTP caching will benefit all users whether they spend a lot of time navigating through your website or if they simply glance at it and return at a later date.

A web server can take advantage of the browser's ability to cache data and use it to improve the repeat request load time. If a user visits the same page twice within one session, there is usually no need to serve them a fresh version of the static files that the page requires. This way, a web server can use the Expires header to notify the web client that it can use the current copy of a component until the specified expiration date. In turn, the browser will then cache this component and only check again for a new version when the user revisits the site or when the component reaches its expiration date. Let's look a little deeper at the exact HTTP request and response that takes place.

Figure 4.2 shows a typical HTTP request that would be made for a CSS file the first time a user visits a website. As you can see in figure 4.3, a response is returned from the server with an Expires header.

The Expires header has been added by the server and will notify the browser that it can cache the component until this expiration date has passed. In the case of figure 4.3 it's only one day, but depending on how often you change your files, you might want to set this date a lot farther in the future. Once a website is stable, you'll be surprised at how seldom the components on a web page change. In chapter 5, we'll take a closer look at the best practices around expiration dates and how far in the future you should set your components to expire. Chapter 5 also goes into detail about the out-of-the-box support that Visual Studio 2012 provides for expiration dates.

In figure 4.3, notice that another type of response header called Cache-Control was returned. The Cache-Control header is an alternative to the Expires header, and it works with time slightly differently. Cache-Control was introduced in HTTP/1.1 and

```
Request URL: http://c516947.r47.cf3.rackcdn.com/combined.css
Request Method: GET
Status Code: ● 200 OK
▼ Request Headers      view source
  Accept: text/css,*/*;q=0.1
  Accept-Charset: ISO-8859-1,utf-8;q=0.7,*;q=0.3
  Accept-Encoding: gzip,deflate,sdch
  Accept-Language: en-GB,en-US;q=0.8,en;q=0.6
  Connection: keep-alive
  Host: c516947.r47.cf3.rackcdn.com
  Referer: http://deanhume.com/
  User-Agent: Mozilla/5.0 (Windows NT 6.1; WOW64) AppleWebKit/537.1
```

Figure 4.2 An HTTP request for a CSS file

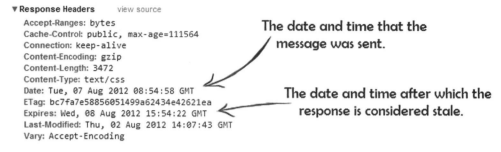

Figure 4.3   An HTTP response for a CSS file

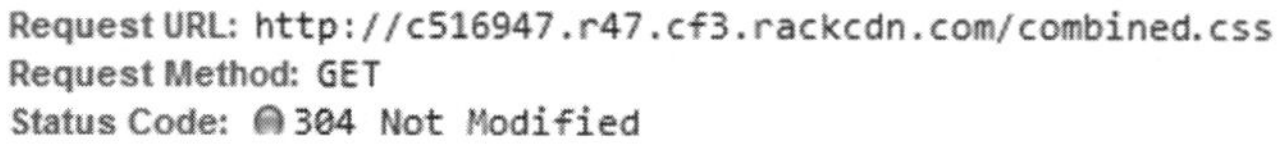

Request URL: http://c516947.r47.cf3.rackcdn.com/combined.css
Request Method: GET
Status Code: ⊜ 304 Not Modified

Figure 4.4   A repeat request for a CSS file which returns a 304 HTTP status

offers more options than the Expires header. In particular, the Expires header uses an exact date and time to specify an expiration; the Cache-Control header uses a max-age in seconds to determine the expiration date from the time it was requested. Both headers can be used together to notify the browser that it needs to cache the component for a certain time and both are perfectly acceptable methods of expiring data. Fortunately for you as a .NET developer, IIS will automatically determine when to use the Expires header or when to use the Cache-Control header. We can easily set the Expires headers in either our IIS web server or within the Web.config file of our application. Once the settings have been applied, they'll all be handled for you by the IIS web server.

We have run through the steps that a browser makes when it requests a component on a web page and it's then told to cache the component, but what about when a second request for a component is made? When a browser makes a repeat request for an object that is still in its cache, it needs to check if anything has changed on the server for that component since it was last requested. If nothing has changed, the server will respond with a 304 HTTP status code notifying the browser that it has not been modified and that it can use the version stored in the browser's cache. The 304 HTTP status code is efficient because the server simply checks the component and returns a small 304 response instead of a full response with the contents of the component. Figure 4.4 shows a repeat request for a CSS file in action.

Notice that this is a repeat request and nothing has changed on the server since the component has been cached, so the server responds with a 304 HTTP status code. It needs to do this to ensure that the file hasn't changed on the server and that it's still okay to use the version that is stored in its cache.

4.2   IIS and HTTP caching

When you're configuring Expires Response headers for your web application, it's important to consider the following information:

- Content that is updated regularly, on a daily or weekly basis, should be configured to expire periodically.
- Content that contains sensitive information that you do not want cached or that is updated frequently should be configured to expire immediately.
- Content that is not expected to change should be configured to expire in approximately one year. You could set the expiration date to ten years in the future, but given the frequency with which users clear and fill their cache, setting an expiration date one year or ten years in the future might not make much difference.

If you're developing a website and have direct access to IIS, it's easy to add an HTTP Expires Response header. We'll apply the changes to the Surf Store application now. First, open up IIS Manager on your computer and navigate to the website that you want to update. In this case, navigate to the Surf Store application, as shown in figure 4.5.

Using IIS, you can choose to apply the Expires headers to individual folders or at the root level of your website. In most cases, you'll want to cache individual folders that contain static files, such as your CSS files, JavaScript files, images, and so on. In the case of the Surf Store application, I am choosing to apply the Expires header to the Styles folder because it contains CSS files that won't change regularly. Once you've selected the folder to which you're applying the caching, double-click HTTP Response Headers in IIS Manager (figure 4.6).

In the Actions pane on the HTTP Response Headers page, click Set Common Headers. A window similar to the one in figure 4.7 will appear in IIS.

Select Expire Web content and choose how long you want the browser to cache the components. For this example, I chose 30 days. There is also the option to

Figure 4.5 Add an Expires header to the Surf Store application by first choosing the website in IIS Manager.

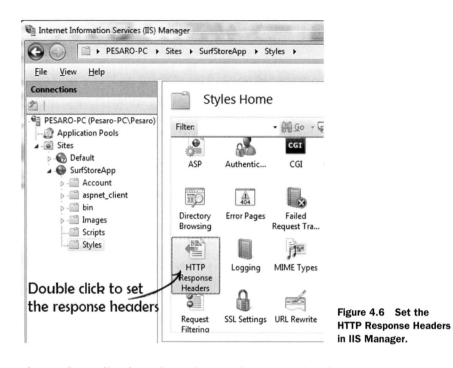

Figure 4.6   Set the HTTP Response Headers in IIS Manager.

choose Immediately and another option to expire the components on a specific date and time.

Using the Yahoo! YSlow tool, you can immediately see the difference after adding the Expires header. If you load up the website and refresh the page, you'll see that all the CSS files in the Styles folder have been set to expire in the future and will not need to fetch the website components again.

In figure 4.8 you can see the two CSS files have an expiration date set from the date the file was requested. Whenever the browser reloads that page, it won't need to request those two files again. If we apply the expiration to the Images and Scripts

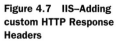

Figure 4.7   IIS–Adding custom HTTP Response Headers

↑ TYPE	SIZE (KB)	URL	EXPIRES (Y/M/D)	RESPONSE TIME (ms)	ETAG	ACTION
⊞ doc (1)	6.2K					
⊞ js (2)	255.2K					
⊟ css (2)	114.2K					
css	99.8K	http://localhost/SurfStoreApp/Styles/bootstrap.css	2012/9/6	0	"20a5738f6970cd1:0"	
css	14.4K	http://localhost/SurfStoreApp/Styles/bootstrap-responsive.css	2012/9/6	0	"26b33347d95dcd1:0"	
⊞ cssimage (1)	79.4K					
⊞ image (6)	686.2K					
⊞ favicon (1)	5.1K					

Figure 4.8 HTTP Response Expires for the CSS files in the Surf Store application

folders, there should be an even more marked improvement in the repeat page load time and primed cache. The weight of the repeat view of the web page in figure 4.9 has significantly reduced in size. It has gone from 1146.6K to 11.4K. We managed to drop over a megabyte from the repeat page load! Imagine saving that amount of data for each new and returning visitor to your site.

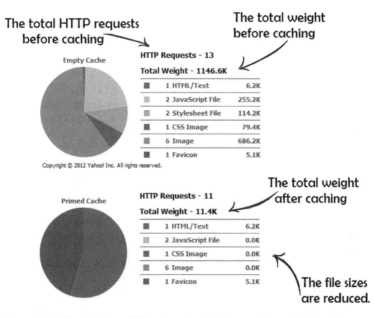

Figure 4.9 The Empty and Primed caches for the sample application after adding Expires headers

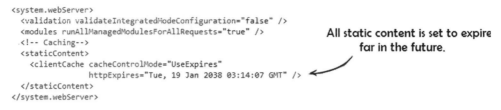

```
<system.webServer>
  <validation validateIntegratedModeConfiguration="false" />
  <modules runAllManagedModulesForAllRequests="true" />
  <!-- Caching-->
  <staticContent>
    <clientCache cacheControlMode="UseExpires"
                 httpExpires="Tue, 19 Jan 2038 03:14:07 GMT" />
  </staticContent>
</system.webServer>
```

All static content is set to expire far in the future.

Figure 4.10   Adding HTTP cache settings in the Web.config

4.3   *Web.config settings*

Much like compression, the expiration details for static content can be set in the Web.config file. This is useful if you work in a shared hosting environment and you don't have access to IIS. You might find that you're working on a website that's hosted with a lot of other websites and your vendor restricts your access to certain elements of the server. You can even achieve the same level of configuration detail you get with IIS when you use the Web.config file.

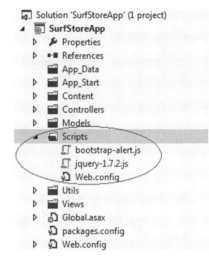

Figure 4.11   The Web.config file is inside the Scripts folder. This will cause the caching to occur at the folder level instead of throughout entire application.

In order to add Expires headers to your application, you'll need to add the lines of code shown in figure 4.10 to your Web.config file.

This code will add an Expires header to all static content that your application processes. This will be handy when you need to apply expiration details across your site, but what about when you need to apply different settings at the folder and file type level? Simply add the code in figure 4.10 to a Web.config at the folder level instead of applying the settings to the Web.config at the root level. Figure 4.11 shows the Web.config file inside the Scripts folder.

By adding a Web.config file to a specific folder, you're ensuring that the caching will occur for that folder instead of the entire application. This can be pretty useful, especially when you need to only cache a certain set of files.

4.4   *Caching considerations*

It would be great if we could cache every component of a web page for a long period of time, but this isn't always possible in most modern web applications. Web applications are dynamic and need to serve up fresh content constantly. That's why it's important to think about the different components that make up a web page and determine each component's caching needs.

Depending on your website's purpose, you may find that you're actually able to cache most of the components for a long period of time. However, what happens when you develop and redeploy changes to these components? Your users might have an old version of a file in their browser's cache even after you've deployed a newer version. Depending on the HTTP response details that are sent back, their browsers might not check with the server for a newer version right away. This could lead to problems if your users are viewing outdated components and information. Keep in mind that as developers, we can easily press CTRL-F5 and force a full browser refresh, but the average website user won't understand that they need to do this.

In chapter 1, you read about the performance cycle and the important role it plays when you're optimizing your website. While reading this chapter, keep in mind the different stages of the performance cycle and where you currently stand. Once you've applied HTTP caching to your website, it's important to monitor any performance changes and any effects this might have on your users. This includes any broken pages that may occur due to incorrect file versions stored in their browser. As a developer, instead of simply adding expiration dates to the web page components, think about your users. How often do you deploy changes? How often do you expect the CSS and JavaScript to change? These are all important questions to ask when analyzing how long to cache components.

To make sure the cache updates instantly when you deploy a new version of a file, the best option is to rename the file. Simply changing the name of the component forces the browser to request the new version of the file, because any references to the old file are lost with its name. For example, if you have a CSS file called site.css and it has an expiration date in a week, the browser won't bother checking for any changes within that week. However, if you change the HTML and update the name of the file to site_v1.css, the browser will be forced to request this new file instead of using the old one from its cache. One downside of this is that you'll need to change the name of your files each and every time you redeploy your application. This type of workaround is known as file versioning or file revving. In chapter 5, we'll look at ways that Visual Studio 2012 automatically versions CSS and JavaScript for you when you combine this technique with file minifying.

4.5 Output caching

We've added HTTP caching to the static components on a web page, but what about dynamic components and especially the HTML web page itself? Fortunately, .NET has a great built-in feature called `OutputCache`. It allows you to cache the contents of a web page based on a number of different factors, such as the parameters passed in, where cache is stored, or how long you'll store the data.

4.5.1 Output caching in an ASP.NET MVC application

In ASP.NET MVC, the output cache enables you to cache the content returned by a controller's action so the same content doesn't need to be generated each and every time the same controller action is invoked. If applied to your controller correctly, it can produce extremely fast repeat load times.

It will be a lot easier to explain how output caching works if we use the Surf Store application as an example. You can enable output caching by adding the `OutputCache` attribute on an individual controller or an entire class. The following listing shows the attribute being added to the sample Surf Store application.

Listing 4.1   Applying output caching to an `Action`

```
[OutputCache(Duration = 100, VaryByParam = "none")]     ◁⎯  Applying the attribute to
public ActionResult Index()                                  the Action on the controller.
{                                                            The output cache will expire
    return View();     ◁⎯  The Action                        in 100 seconds.
}
```

The code in the listing will cache the output of the `Index()` action for 100 seconds. Any additional requests made to the web page within that time frame will receive lightning-fast response times because the content of the web page has been cached on the server.

You can tell the `OutputCache` attribute to adapt its caching activities to meet various parameters. For example, you might want to display personalized content for individual users. Think about the sites, such as Amazon or Facebook, that you log onto daily. These sites need to cache frequently used data and vary the personalized content they display based for each user. The `VaryByParam` property you saw in listing 4.1 helps you accomplish this task. The property can be set to contain a semicolon-separated list of strings to vary the output cache. So depending on the parameters passed in, users will see a different cached version of the website. `VaryByParam` can use the following values:

- *None*—The output will not be cached.
- ***—The cache will vary based on every parameter that is passed in.
- *Any valid query string or POST parameter name*—The cache will vary based on a particular parameter or parameters.

If you used the output cache but didn't vary it based on parameters, you'd find that different users would see the same content, rather than web pages that were personalized for their individual interests. This isn't ideal in modern websites, where content must be dynamic and personalized for each user!

Let's apply a different output cache to the Product page of the Surf Store application. In listing 4.2, the `OutputCache` attribute has been added to the `Action` and is being cached for an hour (or 3600 seconds). We're varying the cache based on the `"category"` parameter, so every time the parameter changes, the server will store a different copy of the action based on the parameter. This `VaryByParam` property is particularly useful when dealing with dynamic web pages because it allows you to serve different content to your users depending on the parameters passed in.

Listing 4.2 Applying `OutputCache` to the Product page

```
[OutputCache(Duration = 3600, VaryByParam = "category")]
public ActionResult Product(string category)
{
List<ProductModel> productModel = new List<ProductModel>();

 // Check if a category was passed in first.
 if (!string.IsNullOrWhiteSpace(category))
 {
   // Retrieve the product images
   Utils.ImageUtils imageUtils = new ImageUtils();
   var productImages = imageUtils.RetrieveProductImages(category);

   // Loop through and add to our Model
   foreach (FileInfo productImage in productImages)
   {
       string imagePath = "~/Content/Images/" +
                          category +
                          "/" +
                          productImage.Name;

       productModel.Add(new ProductModel
                       { ImageDescription = productImage.Name.Replace(
                           productImage.Extension,
                           ""), ImageUrl = imagePath
                       });
   }
 }
return View(productModel);
}
```

Applying the attribute to the Action on the Controller. VaryByParam is used.

The Action Method and the dynamic code that is executed.

The code inside this method is retrieving product details from the database.

As a default setting, the `OutputCache` attribute caches content in three locations: the web server, any proxy servers, and the web browser. In certain circumstances, you might want to specify exactly where the content is cached. You can do so by modifying the `Location` property of the `OutputCache` attribute.

The `Location` property can use the following values:

- *Any*—This is the default setting. The output cache can be stored on either the requesting client or the server.
- *Client*—The output cache is stored on the browser client where the request originated.
- *Downstream*—The output cache can be stored on any device other than the web server.
- *Server*—The output cache is located on the server where the request was processed.
- *None*—The output cache is disabled for the requested page.
- *ServerAndClient*—The output cache can be stored on the server and on the requesting client.

You might use the Location property when you're caching information that's personalized for each user. In that case, it's better not to cache the information on the server, but rather on the client.

The next listing shows how to apply the Location property to the Surf Store application's OutputCache, telling the server where the browser should store the data.

Listing 4.3   Applying the Location setting to the OutputCache

```
[OutputCache(Duration = 86400,
VaryByParam = "category", Location = OutputCacheLocation.Client)]    ◄──────────────┐
public ActionResult Product(string category)                              The OutputCache
{                                                                         attribute has a new field
List<ProductModel> productModel = new List<ProductModel>();    added to it called Location.
                                                                       The Location setting is set to
 // Check if a category was passed in first.                       store the output cache on the client.
 if (!string.IsNullOrWhiteSpace(category))                         The output cache is also being applied
 {                                                                      for a duration of one day and is
   // Retrieve the product images                                       being varied based on the
   Utils.ImageUtils imageUtils = new ImageUtils();                      category parameter.
   var productImages = imageUtils.RetrieveProductImages(category);

   // Loop through and add to our Model
   foreach (FileInfo productImage in productImages)    ◄──┐   The Action and
   {                                                        the dynamic code
       string imagePath = "~/Content/Images/" +            that is executed
                          category + "/" +
                          productImage.Name;

       productModel.Add(new ProductModel {
                                   ImageDescription =
                           productImage.Name.Replace(
                           productImage.Extension, ""
                                                      ),
                           ImageUrl = imagePath });
   }
 }

return View(productModel);
}
```

We added an Expires header to the components of a web page at the beginning of the chapter, and now we've added an Expires header to the web page itself. Let's look at the HTTP response that's returned for the Products page after adding output caching in figure 4.12.

The Expires and Cache-Control headers in figure 4.12 have been set to expire 24 hours from the date of the request. The browser won't bother checking with the server to see if the item has changed, which saves the user another request to the server for the HTML of the page.

4.5.2   *Output caching in an ASP.NET Web Forms application*

Adding output caching to an ASP.NET Web Forms page is similar to an MVC application, except it's applied at the page level. The pages in a Web Forms application will

Cache-Control indicates a max age
of plus one day in the future.

▼ **Query String Parameters**   view URL encoded
   Category: Surfboard
▼ **Response Headers**   view source
   Cache-Control: private, max-age=86400
   Content-Encoding: gzip
   Content-Length: 1380
   Content-Type: text/html; charset=utf-8
   Date: Thu, 09 Aug 2012 07:36:20 GMT
   Expires: Fri, 10 Aug 2012 07:36:20 GMT
   Last-Modified: Thu, 09 Aug 2012 07:36:20 GMT
   Server: Microsoft-IIS/8.0
   Vary: Accept-Encoding

The component is set to expire
plus one day in the future.

**Figure 4.12   Applying output cache to
a web page**

render extremely quickly if output caching has been applied; by adding a few attributes, you'll notice the speed of your application improve instantly. You'll need to add the OutputCache attribute to the top of the web page, as shown in figure 4.13.

The OutputCache attribute applied to the web page will start caching content with an expiration date of one hour. At the moment, it will serve the same content for every user regardless of the output from the server. Earlier, we discussed how a website such as Facebook or Amazon might want to serve different content to different users based on the user parameters passed to the page. The code in figure 4.13 doesn't do that, but you can add that ability with the VaryByParam setting. Let's take a look at this in figure 4.14.

The code in figure 4.14 will cache the details of the Product page for the one hour, or 3600 seconds. The code also has more detail in the VaryByParam setting and will vary its cache according to the category parameter passed to the page. Finally, the cache will be stored on the web server and requesting client (browser) using the Location setting.

The Product page in the Surf Store application will need to serve dynamic content based on each different category that gets passed through, so you're setting the cache with the "category" parameter. For example, if you're on the Product page and see the wetsuits section, a value of "wetsuit" was passed through in the category parameter. To make sure you cache the correct category, you need to make sure the cache is varied based on this parameter.

```
<%@ Page Title="Home Page" Language="C#" MasterPageFile="~/Site.master"
AutoEventWireup="true"CodeBehind="Default.aspx.cs" Inherits="SurfStoreApp.Default" %>
    <%@ OutputCache Duration="3600" VaryByParam="none" %>
```

How long (in seconds) the page
will be cached for

Figure 4.13   Applying OutputCache to an ASP.NET Web Forms page

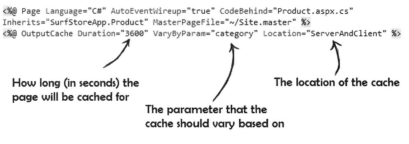

```
<%@ Page Language="C#" AutoEventWireup="true" CodeBehind="Product.aspx.cs"
Inherits="SurfStoreApp.Product" MasterPageFile="~/Site.master" %>
<%@ OutputCache Duration="3600" VaryByParam="category" Location="ServerAndClient" %>
```

How long (in seconds) the
page will be cached for

The parameter that the
cache should vary based on

The location of the cache

Figure 4.14   Applying output cache to the Product page with the `VaryByParam` and `Location` properties

4.6   *The results of HTTP caching*

Now that you've applied caching across our Surf Store application, let's run it through Google PageSpeed and Yahoo! YSlow to see if you've improved its performance score.

In chapter 3, you applied compression to the sample application and bumped the PageSpeed score up to 85. After applying the HTTP caching changes in this chapter, the PageSpeed score has increased to 89, as shown in figure 4.15.

If you run the sample application through the Yahoo! YSlow tool, the results are pretty impressive! See figure 4.16.

The site increased its score from 81 to 91, simply by adding HTTP caching. This is a significant increase, taking you a step closer to achieving a perfect score for the Surf Store application.

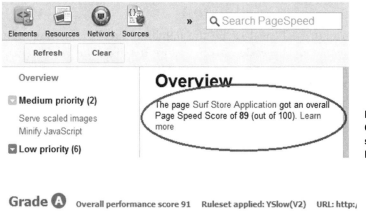

Elements Resources Network Sources

Refresh   Clear

Overview

Overview

Medium priority (2)

Serve scaled images
Minify JavaScript

Low priority (6)

The page Surf Store Application got an overall Page Speed Score of 89 (out of 100). Learn more

Figure 4.15   The Google PageSpeed score after applying HTTP caching

Grade Ⓐ   Overall performance score 91   Ruleset applied: YSlow(V2)   URL: http:.

ALL (23)   FILTER BY: CONTENT (6) | COOKIE (2) | CSS (6) | IMAGES (2) | JAVASCRIPT

A	Make fewer HTTP requests
F	Use a Content Delivery Network (CDN)
A	Avoid empty src or href
A	Add Expires headers
A	Compress components with gzip

Grade A on Add Expires headers

Figure 4.16   The Yahoo! YSlow score after applying HTTP caching

4.7 *Summary*

You've covered a lot of ground in this chapter. You learned how browsers cache the components that make up a web page and how you can harness this cache to reduce repeat HTTP requests. HTTP caching allows you to store static components in the browser's cache, so the next time a user requests any one of these components, it will immediately be retrieved from the cache. This means fewer repeat HTTP requests and a hugely decreased repeat page load time.

IIS plays an important role when it comes to HTTP caching. Using IIS, you have full control of the caching settings you wish to apply to your web page components. Understanding the duration to cache your components for is an important part of web page performance: too long and your users might have content that is out of date, too short and you don't gain the benefits of caching. Using the performance cycle will help you analyze your application as a whole and think about how each component affects the overall load of each page.

In the next chapter, we will look at the new bundling and minification features that have been built into ASP.NET 4.5 and how you can use them to drastically improve your page load times.

Minifying and
bundling static files

5

This chapter covers

- What is minification?
- What is bundling?
- Why should I minify or bundle my static files?
- Minification and bundling in ASP.NET MVC and Web Forms

As a web developer, it's important for you it's important for you to look for imaginative ways to improve your page load times. This often involves reducing the number or weight of the HTTP requests that a user makes when loading a web page. In this chapter we examine bundling and minification, which will help you make fewer HTTP requests and severely reduce the weight of your web pages. ASP.NET 4.5 has fantastic new features that allow you to apply both techniques to your web application easily and automatically. By the end of this chapter, you'll be able to apply these techniques to your web applications in no time!

5.1 What is minification?

Most developer-written JavaScript or CSS contains loads of extra spaces and line breaks that don't get run when the code is executed. Removing these unnecessary spaces and line breaks, a technique known as *minification*, reduces the overall size of the file and, in turn, results in faster page load time, without affecting the integrity of its contents. The code downloads and executes faster, but the code will run in the very same manner—it's an easy win!

When CSS or JavaScript is minified, it starts to lose its readability. It's important to understand that while humans might struggle to read the code, the browser will have no trouble processing it. This is a necessary evil because the removal of whitespace and the obfuscation that results will ultimately help the file load faster. The built-in support for minification that comes with Visual Studio 2012 is also intelligent enough that while you're developing you'll be able to see the full, unminified code. When you run your website in Release mode, the code will automatically get minified on the fly for you.

In the Surf Store application, we've added HTTP caching and compression, which has drastically improved the page load speed. But if we run the sample application as it stands against the Google PageSpeed tool, there are still things that need to be done in order to improve our PageSpeed score. One of the most important things you can do to boost page load time is minify JavaScript (figure 5.1).

Overview

▼ **Medium priority (2)**

Serve scaled images
Minify JavaScript

▼ **Low priority (6)**

Minify CSS
Defer parsing of JavaScript
Optimize the order of styl...
Optimize images

Figure 5.1   The remaining improvements that need to be implemented, according to the Google PageSpeed tool

If we take a typical CSS file and minify it, the results compared to the original version are very different in both appearance and file size. The next listing shows a CSS snippet before it's been minified.

Listing 5.1   CSS code before minification

```
/*This is a comment*/
h1 {
  font-size: 30px;
  line-height: 36px;
}

h1 small {
  font-size: 18px;
}

h2 {
  font-size: 24px;
  line-height: 36px;
}

h2 small {
  font-size: 18px;
}

h3 {
  font-size: 18px;
  line-height: 27px;
}
```

◁─┐ **Standard CSS formatting
    with line breaks and spaces**

```
h3 small {
  font-size: 14px;
}
```

As you can see, the CSS contains unnecessary spaces, tabs, and line breaks. Although this makes the code a lot easier to read and prettier to the human eye, ultimately it adds extra weight to the overall size of the file. The next listing shows you what the code looks like after it's been minified.

Listing 5.2   CSS code after minification

```
h1{#1 font-size:30px;line-height:36px}h1 small{font-size:18px}h2{font-
size:24px;line-height:36px}h2 small{font-size:18px}h3{font-size:18px;
line-height:27px}h3 small{font-size:14px}
```

Differences between the two listings are visible immediately. The code has no spaces, and the comments, tabs, and line breaks have been removed, making the code snippet a lot smaller. These two examples use a small piece of code, but imagine the difference this could make if minification were applied to all the CSS and JavaScript in your application.

JavaScript can be minified and obfuscated to reduce the file size even further. Look at the following JavaScript code before it has been minified.

Listing 5.3   JavaScript code before minification

```
$(document).ready(function () {
    //Detect enter key
    $('#barcodeValue').keyup(function (event) {          The code contains comments
        if (event.keyCode == 13) {                       and unnecessary whitespace.
            validateString($("#barcodeValue").val(),
                $("#barcodeType option:selected").val());
        }                                                The method names
    });                                                  are longer than they
                                                         need to be, adding
    // Hide the value textbox                            weight to the file.
    $("#barcodeValue").hide();

    // Drop down changed
    $("#barcodeType").change(function () {
        // show the value textbox
        $("#barcodeValue").show();

        // Prepend the textbox if necessary
        shouldPrepend();
    });
});
```

The code in the next listing has been obfuscated and minified, and there's a big difference in the readability of the file when you compare it to listing 5.3. Although the minified code isn't easy on the human eye, it's perfectly acceptable to use the compressed version on the server after development has been completed.

Listing 5.4   JavaScript code after minification

```
$(document).ready(function(){$("#barcodeValue").keyup(function(a){if(a.key
Code==13){validateString($("#barcodeValue").val(),$("#barcodeType
option:selected").val())}});$("#barcodeValue").hide();$("#CreateButton")
.hide();$("#alertBox").hide();$("#progressBar").hide();$("#infoLink").hide();
$("#barcodeType").change(function(){$("#barcodeValue").show();$("#CreateButton")
.show();shouldPrepend()})});
```

Developers often like to keep two versions of their code: one for debugging and one for deployment in a live environment. When you visit the jQuery website, you'll notice that there's an option to download a minified version of jQuery. The filename will often end in .min.js, which has become the standard method of naming the files. The unminified version will be named something like jquery-1.8.0.js, while the minified version will be called jquery-1.8.0.min.js. This makes it easy to identify the files while you're developing your application.

Table 5.1 contains a list of common JavaScript and CSS frameworks and the differences in their file sizes before and after minification.

Table 5.1   Common JavaScript and CSS frameworks and their minification file size savings

Filenames	File size before minification	File size after minification	File size savings
jQuery	225.78 KB	93.28 KB	58.68%
jQuery Mobile	240 KB	91 KB	62%
Twitter Bootstrap CSS	98 KB	80 KB	19%

As you can see from table 5.1, the size savings vary considerably across the different files, and is probably due to factors such as whitespace, comments, and line breaks. If we can achieve this level of file size savings with no functional changes to our code, it seems obvious that minifying the code is a free and easy win.

Later in this chapter we're going to automatically apply minification to the files in the Surf Store application with the new built-in features in ASP.NET 4.5 and Visual Studio 2012. If you prefer to minify your files manually, there are many online tools that allow you to do so.

The online YUI compressor uses the Yahoo! YUI compressor to easily minify both JavaScript and CSS. All you have to do is paste the contents of the file into the textbox and you'll be presented with an option to download the minified file. The web application is available at http://refresh-sf.com/yui/.

Another tool for use with JavaScript is the Google Closure Compiler. It's used in many of Google's JavaScript apps, including Gmail, Google Web Search, Google Maps, and Google Docs. An online version of the tool is available at closure-compiler.appspot.com.

There are many other tools available on the web, but keep in mind that each might use a different algorithm and a slightly different method of minification. What's important is that they all use minification techniques that significantly reduce the size of these files. The only downside to using these online tools is that the minification process is manual; you'll have to upload each version of your CSS and JavaScript and wait for the download before adding it back into your project. Later in the chapter, we're going to explore the built-in minification support that Visual Studio 2012 offers, which will automatically handle this for you.

5.2　What is bundling?

A technique that works well with minification is *bundling*. You might find that your web pages contain references to many CSS and JavaScript files. While this makes our lives easier as we're developing our websites, having more than one CSS or JavaScript file once the code goes into production isn't always ideal. More file references mean more HTTP requests, and in our quest to improve the overall speed of a website, we need to reduce the number of requests that a web page makes. The easiest thing to do is to combine all of the JavaScript into one file, and combine all of the CSS into another file. This technique is known as bundling. If you had four JavaScript files before bundling, you would have had four HTTP requests. If the JavaScript files are bundled, you'll only have one HTTP request, which will speed up your website considerably!

In a standard web page, each component is requested separately by the browser and returned by the server. Once the code reaches the browser, it doesn't care if it's neatly formatted and split into a logical order. The browser will execute the code regardless and by bundling the files we're making it a lot quicker for the browser to receive the code that it needs to execute. Bundling is easy to implement and it seems a waste not to take advantage of this simple technique to speed up your web pages. Utilizing bundling and minifying together allows you to amplify those savings even more.

5.3　New bundling and minifying features in ASP.NET 4.5

In this section you're going to apply bundling and minification to our Surf Store application. Some great features included in the release of Visual Studio 2012 will boost and improve your page speed. You're going to focus on the bundling and minification features that can be found under the System.Web.Optimization namespace.

This namespace allows you to bundle and minify all of the JavaScript and CSS in the project folder simply by sending a URL request to a preset virtual folder path. This code will work in both ASP.NET Web Forms and ASP.NET MVC, and is included automatically when you create a project in Visual Studio 2012. As you can see in figure 5.2, it can be found in the Solution Explorer under the App_Start folder.

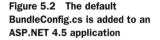

Figure 5.2　The default BundleConfig.cs is added to an ASP.NET 4.5 application

NOTE   It should be noted that if you choose an *empty* ASP.NET MVC project template, you won't find this class in your project. It is the simplest type of ASP.NET project and it doesn't contain the full set of classes that you might need.

This `BundleConfig` class contains code that allows you to create Script and Style bundles that will bundle and minify the files. You're going to run through an example in both ASP.NET MVC and Web Forms, but first it's important to understand how each request is handled by ASP.NET.

In order to create a Script bundle, you'll need to instantiate it by referencing a virtual path to the files that you want to bundle. The following listing contains code that you'll need to implement or replace in the `RegisterBundles()` method of the `BundleConfig` class.

Listing 5.5   Creating Script and Style bundles

```
public static void RegisterBundles(BundleCollection bundles)
    {
        bundles.Add(new StyleBundle("~/Styles/Css").Include(      ◁─┤   A Style bundle
            "~/Content/Css/bootstrap.css",                              that minifies
            "~/Content/Css/bootstrap-responsive.css"                    and bundles
                ));                                                      two CSS files

        bundles.Add(new ScriptBundle("~/Scripts/Js").Include(     ◁─┐
            "~/Scripts/bootstrap-alert.js",
            "~/Scripts/jquery-1.7.2.js"                   A Script bundle that
                ));                                       minifies and bundles
    }                                                     two JavaScript files
```

The first virtual path referenced in the `ScriptBundle` is a reference to a file that doesn't exist and can therefore be anything. In this case, I have pointed it to "~/Styles/Css". The code will then service any requests to the path provided. For example, if we want to apply this to CSS, we request:

```
<link href="/Styles/Css" rel="stylesheet">
```

As the website compiles and runs for the first time, ASP.NET will search the directory shown in the previous listing, and it will bundle and minify all the CSS files it finds. When the virtual directory for the bundle is requested, it will send back a single HTTP response with all of the CSS combined and minified together. The same piece of code can be applied to all JavaScript files in a directory by simply changing the path to:

```
<script src="/Scripts/Js" type="text/javascript"></script>
```

By referencing the files, ASP.NET 4.5 will generate a reference to the bundled and minified CSS and JavaScript files in the respective directories. For example, instead of seeing two CSS file references in the HTML, we now see only one combined file to give us only one HTTP request. Figure 5.3 shows the data that is inside the newly combined file.

The code in figure 5.3 has been word wrapped and cut short to make it easier to read, but you can see there are no spaces and the code is pretty difficult to read. Visual

```
article,aside,details,figcaption,figure,footer,header,hgroup
block;*display:inline;*zoom:1}audio:not([controls]){display:
dotted #333;outline:5px auto -webkit-focus-ring-color;outlin
align:baseline}sup{top:-.5em}sub{bottom:-.25em}img{max-width
width:none}button,input,select,textarea{margin:0;font-size:1
inner,input::-moz-focus-inner{padding:0;border:0}button,inpu
appearance:button}input[type="search"]{-webkit-box-sizing:co
appearance:textfield}input[type="search"]::-webkit-search-de
appearance:none}textarea{overflow:auto;vertical-
align:top}.clearfix{*zoom:1}.clearfix:before,.clearfix:after
shadow:none;background-color:transparent;border:0}.input-blo
box;-ms-box-sizing:border-box;box-sizing:border-box}body{mar
height:18px;color:#333;background-color:#fff}a{color:#08c;te
left:-20px;*zoom:1}.row:before,.row:after{display:table;cont
.container,.navbar-fixed-bottom
```

**Figure 5.3   A bundled and minified file after applying the new features in the
System.Web.Optimization namespace**

Studio has taken care of the hard work for us, and it only took a matter of minutes to
implement this change. If you mistakenly specify a path of a script file or CSS file that
doesn't exist, the framework will gracefully handle it for you and not throw any errors.
You won't get any runtime exceptions and the framework will continue to bundle and
minify the rest of the files.

The great thing about this new feature is that you don't need to run any tools or
manually minify or bundle these files—it happens automatically when you run your
application. You're also in total control as you can switch it on and off as you need it.
This quick change easily handles bundling and minification for you and it's definitely
a step in the right direction.

> **NOTE**   This optimization will only occur under Release mode. You may notice
> that the files you've requested are not being bundled while you're develop-
> ing. By default, bundling is automatically disabled under Debug mode to
> make life easier for the developer to read and update the code. Once you
> compile your application under Release mode, the optimizations take place
> and bundling is enabled. If you need to test this feature while in Debug
> mode, you can temporarily override it by setting `BundleTable.Enable-`
> `Optimizations = true` in your BundleConfig.cs file. This will minify and bun-
> dle your files while in Debug mode.

In chapter 4 we covered Expires Headers and how they notify the browser to cache
static resources for a specified duration. Before a web page requests a resource, the
browser first checks its cache to see if it has a resource with a matching URL. This can
sometimes be problematic because as you're developing and releasing new changes to
your application, your users might have older versions of these files in their browser's
cache. One option was to force refresh of the cache using file versioning, or file revving, and this appends a query string onto the end of the filename.

```
<link type="text/css" rel="stylesheet" href="/Styles/bootstrap.css?v=1.1">
```

ASP.NET 4.5 automatically adds a hashcode to the query parameter for you.

```
<link type="text/css" rel="stylesheet" href="/Styles/
    bootstrap.css?v=ABnfFdbAnRuas7H">
```

If you updated the contents of one of the files and they are bundled using the new optimization feature, a new hashcode will be appended to the end of the filename automatically. This requires no extra code and is simply handled for you.

As long as the contents of the bundle don't change, the ASP.NET application will request the bundle using this hashcode. If any file in the bundle changes, the ASP.NET optimization framework will generate a new hashcode, guaranteeing that browser requests for the bundle will get the latest bundle and force a refresh of the cache. Bundles also set the HTTP Expires header to expire one year from when the bundle is created. This means you'll automatically get the benefits of HTTP caching when creating your bundles.

5.4   *Utilizing bundling in ASP.NET MVC*

You've learned a bit about the process of bundling in Visual Studio 2012, and now it's time to dive into specific coding examples. This section covers the steps that you'll need to perform in order to enable bundling in your ASP.NET MVC web application. You'll be using the Surf Store application as a reference for this example.

When you create an MVC 4 project in Visual Studio 2012, you'll be presented with a screen similar to the image in figure 5.4 which shows the available project templates.

Once you've chosen your project template, a BundleConfig.cs file will appear in your App_Start folder of your project. As already mentioned, this can be used to set the Script and Style bundles and their associated paths.

The following listing shows how a default Global.asax file will look when it contains a reference to the `BundleConfig` class.

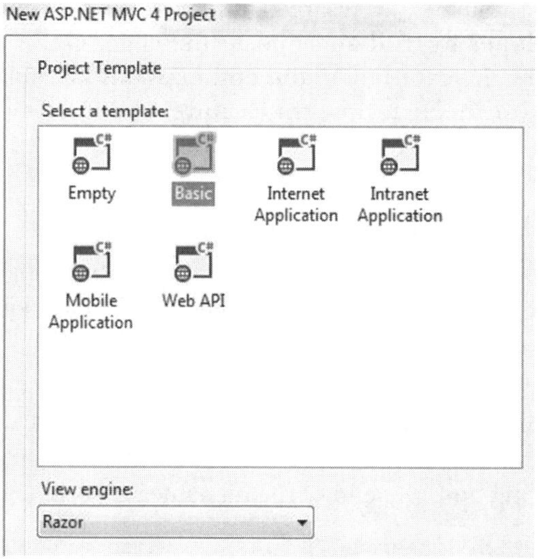

Figure 5.4   Creating a new MVC 4
project in Visual Studio 2012

Listing 5.6   The Global.asax file

```
protected void Application_Start()
{
    AreaRegistration.RegisterAllAreas();

    WebApiConfig.Register(GlobalConfiguration.Configuration);
    FilterConfig.RegisterGlobalFilters(GlobalFilters.Filters);
    RouteConfig.RegisterRoutes(RouteTable.Routes);

    BundleConfig.RegisterBundles(BundleTable.Bundles);
}
```

> References the bundles you'll set up in the **BundleConfig** class in the **App_Start** folder.

The Global.asax file will register the bundles that you're about to set up. The next listing contains the code needed to set up your bundles in the `BundleConfig` class.

Listing 5.7   The `BundleConfig` class for the SurfStore application

> Adds a new list of JavaScript files to the bundles in the application. You can then reference the Script bundle by its virtual path: "~/Scripts/Js".

```
public class BundleConfig
{
    public static void RegisterBundles(BundleCollection bundles)
    {
        bundles.Add(new ScriptBundle("~/Scripts/Js").Include(
            "~/Scripts/bootstrap-alert.js",
            "~/Scripts/jquery-1.7.2.js"
                ));

        bundles.Add(new StyleBundle("~/Styles/Css").Include(
            "~/Content/Css/bootstrap.css",
            "~/Content/Css/bootstrap-responsive.css"
                ));
    }
}
```

> Adds a new list of CSS files to the bundles in the application. Once this is in place, you can reference the Style bundle by its virtual path: "~/Styles/Css".

The previous listing shows how the different bundles in an application can be set up. You're able to add multiple bundles to the `BundleConfig` class, then call them by their virtual path. Finally, you need to add these bundles and their virtual paths to the Layout view. Navigate to the _Layout.cshtml master view file in your Solution Explorer, as shown in figure 5.5.

> ▷ 🗀 Utils
> ◢ 🗀 Views
>   ◢ 🗀 Shared
>   [@] _Layout.cshtml

Figure 5.5   The Layout view in an MVC project

You're using the JavaScript and CSS file references from listing 5.7. Open the view and reference the JavaScript and CSS files using the default bundles. Two new HTML helpers have been introduced in the ASP.NET 4.5 framework: @Styles and @Scripts. Both, as shown in the next listing, can be used as an easy way to render the full HTML you need to reference your scripts and styles.

Listing 5.8   Layout.cshtml with bundling and minification applied

> The updated JavaScript path using the Scripts HTML helper. This will bundle and minify all JavaScript files in this directory.

> The updated CSS path using the Styles HTML helper. This will bundle and minify all CSS files in this directory.

```
<!DOCTYPE html>
<html lang="en">
<head>
    <asp:ContentPlaceHolder runat="server" ID="HeadContent">
        <meta charset="utf-8">
        <title>Surf Store Application</title>
        <link rel="shortcut icon"
href="@Url.Content("~/Content/Images/favicon.ico")" />
        <meta name="viewport" content="width=device-width,
initial-scale=1.0">
        <meta name="description" content="">
        <meta name="author" content="">
          @System.Web.Optimization.Styles.Render("~/Styles/Css")
          @System.Web.Optimization.Scripts.Render ("~/Scripts/js")
```

When the application is compiled and run, the HTML helpers in the previous listing will produce HTML similar to that in figure 5.6.

The code in figure 5.6 will bundle and minify all the CSS and JavaScript files in their respective directories. Notice the hashtag appended to the end of the filename. This hashtag is dynamic and will change only when the contents of the file change. By appending a different hashtag to the filename each time the contents change, you're effectively ensuring that your users will receive a fresh copy of the contents each time they visit your website.

If you run the page against the developer tools in Internet Explorer, you can immediately see the differences. As shown in figure 5.7, the page requested four static files previously, which meant four HTTP requests.

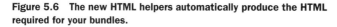

The hashtag

```
<link href="/Styles/Css?v=yB39lqPrSd t" rel="stylesheet"/>
<script src="/Scripts/Js?v=W2Ez5WlK4G4VBlfrDtiYKSCYZAvSTd."></script>
```

The path reference

Figure 5.6   The new HTML helpers automatically produce the HTML required for your bundles.

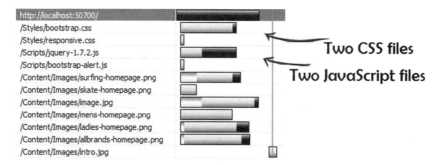

Figure 5.7   CSS and JavaScript before bundling and minification in ASP.NET MVC. Notice that there are four HTTP requests: two for the CSS and two for the JavaScript.

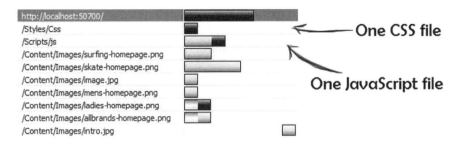

Figure 5.8   CSS and JavaScript after bundling and minification in ASP.NET MVC. There are only two requests for the CSS and the JavaScript.

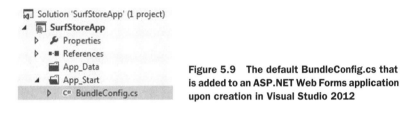

Figure 5.9   The default BundleConfig.cs that is added to an ASP.NET Web Forms application upon creation in Visual Studio 2012

After applying the changes to the Layout view, the HTTP requests have been reduced and you can see the virtual paths that you referenced in the `BundleConfig` class in figure 5.8.

Applying bundling to your ASP.NET MVC application has been made really easy with the new features in Visual Studio 2012. The new HTML helpers work with both the Razor and ASPX view engines. They are easy to use and don't require major changes to your existing development workflow.

5.5   *Utilizing bundling in ASP.NET Web Forms*

In the .NET 4.5 framework, ASP.NET MVC and ASP.NET Web Forms benefit from the System.Web.Optimization namespace. Applying bundling and minification in ASP.NET Web Forms is an easy process that is handled when you create a Web Forms project in Visual Studio 2012. You'll notice in figure 5.9 that a BundleConfig.cs file has been created under the App_Start folder.

The Global.asax class file in your Solution Explorer will contain the following lines under the `Application_Start` method. The listing shows how a default Global.asax file will look when it contains a reference to BundleConfig.cs class file.

Listing 5.9   The Global.asax file

References the bundles that you will set up in the BundleConfig class under the App_Start folder.

```
public class Global : HttpApplication
{
    void Application_Start(object sender, EventArgs e)
    {
        // Code that runs on application startup
        BundleConfig.RegisterBundles(BundleTable.Bundles);
        BundleTable.EnableOptimizations = true;
    }
}
```

If you need to test the bundling and minifying features while in Debug mode, simply add this line to force the enabling of the optimizations.

The Global.asax file in the listing will register the bundles you're about to set up. It will do so as the application starts for the first time, so they're ready to use as and when you need them. The following listing shows how to set up the correct bundles in the BundleConfig class.

Listing 5.10   The BundleConfig class

```
public class BundleConfig
{
    public static void RegisterBundles(BundleCollection bundles)
    {
        bundles.Add(new ScriptBundle("~/Scripts/Js").Include(
            "~/Scripts/bootstrap-alert.js",
            "~/Scripts/jquery-1.7.2.js"
                ));

        bundles.Add(new StyleBundle("~/Styles/Css").Include(
            "~/Content/Css/bootstrap.css",
            "~/Content/Css/bootstrap-responsive.css"
                ));
    }
}
```

Adds a new list of JavaScript files to the bundles in the application. You can then reference the Script bundle by its virtual path: "~/Scripts/Js".

Adds a new list of CSS files to the bundles in the application. You can then reference the Style bundle by its virtual path: "~/Styles/Css".

The listing contains the code that will initialize the bundles for the JavaScript and CSS files. By using the BundleConfig class, you're able to specify which files will get minified and bundled when the application starts. Next, navigate to the Site.Master file in the Solution Explorer (figure 5.10).

Figure 5.10   The Site.Master file in an ASP.NET Web Forms application

Open the master page and reference the JavaScript and CSS files using the default bundles. Two new HTML helpers have been introduced in the ASP.NET 4.5 framework: Styles and Scripts. They can both be used to render the full HTML that you need to reference your scripts and styles. This listing contains the code you need to apply to the Surf Store application.

Listing 5.11   Site.Master page with bundling and minification applied

```
<!DOCTYPE html>
<html lang="en">
<head>
    <asp:ContentPlaceHolder runat="server" ID="HeadContent">
        <meta charset="utf-8">
        <title>Surf Store Application</title>
```

Updated CSS path using the Styles HTML helper. If the application is in Release mode, it will bundle and minify all CSS files in this directory.

```
        <link rel="shortcut icon" href="<%= "Images/favicon.ico" %>" />
        <meta name="viewport" content="width=device-width,
initial-scale=1.0">
        <meta name="description" content="">
        <meta name="author" content="">
        <%= Styles.Render("~/Styles/Css")%>
        <%= Scripts.Render("~/Scripts/Js")%>
```

The updated JavaScript path using the Scripts HTML helper. If the application is in Release mode, it will bundle and minify all JavaScript files in this directory.

The Scripts and Styles HTML helpers will minify and bundle the code when you're in Release mode. When you're in Debug mode, the helpers will simply return all of the JavaScript and CSS in individual HTML tags. When the application is compiled and run in Release mode, the code in listing 5.11 will produce HTML similar to that in figure 5.11.

The code in listing 5.10 will bundle and minify all the CSS and JavaScript files in the respective directories. Notice the hashtag that has been appended to the end of the filename. This hashtag will be dynamic and only change when the contents of the file change. By appending a different hashtag to the filename each time the contents change, you're effectively ensuring that your users will receive a fresh copy of the contents.

If you run the application and check the Network Traffic tab in Internet Explorer's developer tools (figure 5.12), you can immediately see the differences. The page previously requested four static files, which meant four HTTP requests.

After applying the changes to the Site.Master page, the HTTP requests have been reduced and you can see the virtual paths that you referenced in the `BundleConfig` class (figure 5.13).

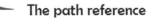

The hashtag

```
<link href="/Styles/Css?v=yB39lqPrSd t" rel="stylesheet"/>
<script src="/Scripts/Js?v=W2Ez5WlK4G4VBlfrDtiYKSCYZAvSTd."></script>
```

The path reference

Figure 5.11   The new HTML helpers automatically produce the HTML required for your bundles

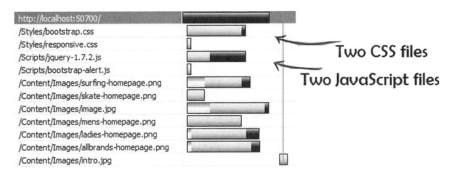

Figure 5.12   CSS and JavaScript before bundling and minification in ASP.NET Web Forms. Notice that there are four HTTP requests: two for the CSS and two for the JavaScript.

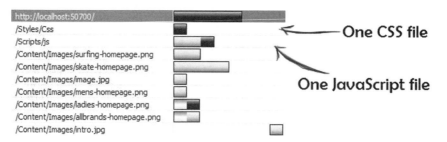

Figure 5.13   CSS and JavaScript after bundling and minification in ASP.NET Web Forms. There are only two requests for the CSS and the JavaScript.

Adding these changes to the sample Surf Store application has been quick and easy. Although you've run through standard implementations using bundling support in ASP.NET 4.5, I really like that this feature supports a rich extensibility API that enables you to customize the bundling settings to your personal needs.

5.6   The results

It's worth mentioning the steps you've taken this far to improve the page speed of the Surf Store application. As of now, you've added:

- Compression (Gzip): Chapter 3
- HTTP caching (HTTP Expires): Chapter 4
- Output caching: Chapter 4
- Minification and bundling: Chapter 5

All of these features can and should be applied together to achieve the maximum effect on the improvement of your overall page load time. Is it worth adding compression if you're minifying the file or vice versa? Definitely, because the files can still be compressed further after you've minified them.

By adding HTTP caching on top of this, you're also reducing the number of HTTP requests that the user's browser needs to make when visiting your website. All of these techniques are stacking up on one another to produce a faster, leaner, and more efficient website with extremely fast load times (figure 5.14).

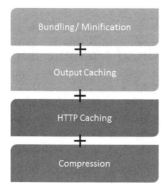

Figure 5.14   The techniques that you've learned so far are all stacking up to build a high-speed, efficient website.

Figure 5.15 The Google PageSpeed score after applying minification and bundling

Minifying the CSS and JavaScript in the Surf Store application has been an easy task using the new features built into ASP.NET 4.5. You were able to minify and bundle multiple files together, which had a big impact on your overall page speed. The Surf Store application's Google PageSpeed score was 89 at the end of chapter 4. If we test the Surf Store application after minification and bundling (figure 5.15) you can see even more improvement. The PageSpeed score has jumped to 93.

Our minification and bundling efforts show good results when you run the website against the Yahoo! YSlow tool (figure 5.16), as well. Our performance went from a score of 90 to 91 and bumped us up to a grade A!

The changes have significantly improved our page weight and the number of HTTP requests. Figure 5.17 shows a before and after result.

You're slowly reducing the number of HTTP requests that the sample Surf Store application needs to make. These changes have not affected the overall integrity of the code, but have boosted and improved the performance and load times of the application.

Grade Ⓐ Overall performance score 91   Ruleset applied: YSlow(V2)

<u>ALL (23)</u>   FILTER BY: <u>CONTENT (6)</u> | <u>COOKIE (2)</u> | <u>CSS (6)</u> | <u>IMAGES (2)</u> |

A	Make fewer HTTP requests
F	<u>Use a Content Delivery Network (CDN)</u>
A	Avoid empty src or href
A	Add Expires headers
A	Compress components with gzip
B	Put CSS at top
A	Put JavaScript at bottom

Figure 5.16 The Yahoo! YSlow score after applying bundling and minification

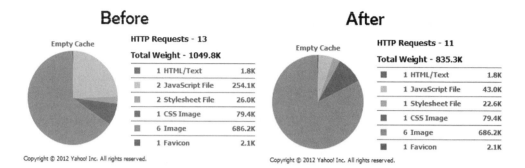

Figure 5.17   The overall page weight and number of HTTP requests before and after minification and bundling

In figure 5.17, the chart on the left shows a total of 13 HTTP requests and a total page weight of 1049.8K. The chart on the right, after you've applied minification and bundling, tells a different story. You've reduced the number of HTTP requests to 11 and reduced the total page weight to 835.3K. This is pretty impressive and improvements were all made with the built-in support that ASP.NET 4.5 offers. Imagine what these changes could do for your web application!

5.7   Summary

In this chapter you've learned the all-important aspects of minifying and bundling your CSS and JavaScript files. In doing so, you've drastically reduced the size of the requested files. You've also reduced the number of requests each web page needs to make, giving you a two-way win.

There are new optimization features in ASP.NET 4.5 that are available with out-of-the-box support in Visual Studio 2012. They make it easy for you as an ASP.NET developer to apply minification and bundling to your web application.

It may seem like such a subtle difference when using the techniques that we covered in this chapter, but minification and bundling can seriously improve your page load times and save on the number of bytes your users need to download. It takes no time at all to apply it, and your users will definitely benefit from this change. Over the past few chapters, you've been building a basic foundation of simple techniques that are beginning to add up to a substantial toolkit. Together, these optimization techniques form the basis of a highly optimized website. In the next chapter, we begin to dive into HTML optimization techniques and look at how you can harness the power of HTML5 to improve the performance of your web applications.

HTML optimization tips

This chapter covers

- Positioning CSS and JavaScript in a web page for best performance
- How CSS and JavaScript placement affects rendering
- The impact of duplicate scripts
- HTML5 optimization techniques

This chapter contains a collection of HTML best practices and tips that will improve the performance of your website. Some tips may seem like small changes, but they'll go a long way toward improving the overall load time and responsiveness of your website. We'll cover the optimal position in the HTML to place CSS and JavaScript, as well as the order in which they should appear.

You'll learn a few HTML5 techniques and how you can apply these techniques to your application to achieve quicker load times. This chapter builds on the Surf Store application that you've been using thus far, and applies HTML5 techniques in different scenarios.

6.1   *Where to position CSS and JavaScript in a web page to achieve the best performance*

When you start building a new website, you may not be concerned with the order or location of the style sheets on your web page. However, their order and location play an important role in the way a browser renders a web page.

6.1.1   *CSS*

The position of CSS in an HTML document has less to do with download times, and more to do with how the browser reacts and renders the page. It's all about perceived speed for the user!

Listing 6.1   Style Sheets located at the bottom of the page

```
<!DOCTYPE html>
<html lang="en">
<head>
        <meta charset="utf-8">
        <title>Surf Store Application</title>
        <link rel="shortcut icon" href="Images/favicon.ico" />
        <meta name="description" content="">
        <meta name="author" content="">
 <script src="Scripts/jquery-1.7.2.js"></script>          ◁──┐
</head>
<body>
 <link href="Styles/bootstrap.css" rel="stylesheet" />          ◁──
 <link href="Styles/bootstrap-responsive.css" rel="stylesheet" />   ◁──
</body>
</html>
```

The JavaScript is located in the `<head>` tag of the document.

CSS located at the bottom of the page is not ideal, because it blocks the rendering of a web page.

In a typical HTML web page the JavaScript is located in the `<head>` tag of the document and the CSS is in the body of the page. Placing CSS at the bottom of a web page is not the optimal position because browsers block the rendering of a web page until all external style sheets have been downloaded. This means that if your style sheet is located at the bottom of a web page, it will block everything else from loading and you might see a blank white screen for a short while. This is not good. Figure 6.1 shows how the location of CSS on a web page affects the way a page renders.

It may seem as if the waterfall chart in figure 6.1 represents the best-case scenario for page rendering, but nothing will be visible on the web page until after the CSS has been downloaded and parsed. Putting the CSS near the bottom of the document prevents progressive rendering in many browsers. *Progressive rendering* means the web page begins to appear and the text can be read even before all the text or images have been completely downloaded. Most browsers block rendering to avoid having to redraw elements of the page if the CSS changes. Some browsers will even leave the user with a blank white page while they are waiting.

In fact, the best place to put your style sheets is in the document `<head>` tag. If style sheets are downloaded and parsed first, the browser is able to render the page progressively instead of blocking the rendering until the CSS has finished loading. By

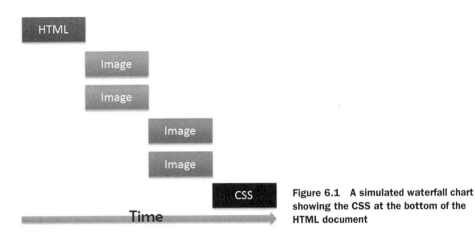

Figure 6.1 A simulated waterfall chart showing the CSS at the bottom of the HTML document

positioning the CSS in the document <head> tag, you're also allowing the browser to begin displaying whatever content it has as soon as possible.

Listing 6.2 shows the CSS located in the document <head> tag in the Surf Store application. The same principle applies to inline style blocks, which can cause reflows and shifting of content. Reflow is the name of the web browser process for recalculating the positions and geometries of elements in a web page. Reflows block the browser while they try to recalculate the position of elements on a web page. The following listing is a web page from the Surf Store application, and you can see the small snippet of inline CSS that is necessary to include a visual header on the page. This inline style tag needs to reside in the document head for the best performance.

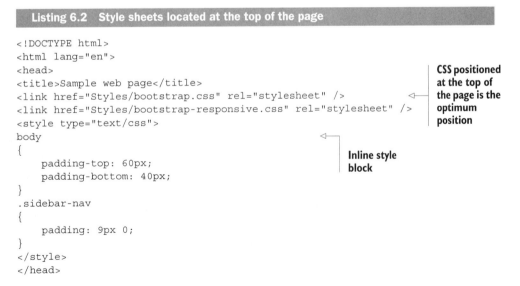

Listing 6.2 Style sheets located at the top of the page

```
<!DOCTYPE html>
<html lang="en">
<head>
<title>Sample web page</title>
<link href="Styles/bootstrap.css" rel="stylesheet" />
<link href="Styles/bootstrap-responsive.css" rel="stylesheet" />
<style type="text/css">
body
{
    padding-top: 60px;
    padding-bottom: 40px;
}
.sidebar-nav
{
    padding: 9px 0;
}
</style>
</head>
```

CSS positioned at the top of the page is the optimum position

Inline style block

Figure 6.2 shows the CSS positioned at the top of the HTML document. You may not notice faster download times by placing the CSS at the top of your web page, but

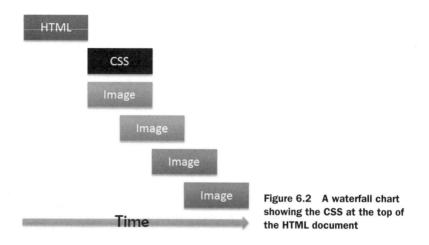

Figure 6.2   A waterfall chart showing the CSS at the top of the HTML document

this will at least allow the user to see something on the page while the rest of the page renders.

6.1.2   JavaScript

The location and order of JavaScript can also have a positive and negative effect on the way a page is rendered. If CSS needs to be in the document head, you might presume that your JavaScript should go there too. In fact, the best place for JavaScript is at the bottom of a web page because JavaScript blocks the browser's ability to download components in parallel. In other words, it blocks progressive rendering for all content in the web page that's placed after the JavaScript. If you place the JavaScript at the bottom of a web page, the content above the script will be rendered faster.

This may seem like a contradiction. You moved your CSS to the document head to allow progressive rendering but you place your JavaScript at the bottom of the web page to allow progressive rendering. Why? So the JavaScript is guaranteed to be executed in the proper order. For example, if code that required the jQuery library is executed before the jQuery library is actually downloaded, all sorts of errors would occur.

Moving the JavaScript to the bottom of a web page means there is more content above the script, and that content will be rendered sooner rather than later. Browsers run JavaScript in a single thread, so if a script is executing, the browser might not be able to start other downloads. If you move the JavaScript to the bottom of the page, the other downloads on the page are allowed to complete without any blocks. It appears faster visually, but the download times also reflect a performance improvement. Figure 6.3 shows what a waterfall chart would look like if you placed the JavaScript at the top of the page versus placing it at the bottom of the page.

In the top waterfall chart, you can see that the images and all other components are waiting for the JavaScript to finish downloading before they can start rendering. This isn't ideal. The second waterfall chart shows what happens when you move the

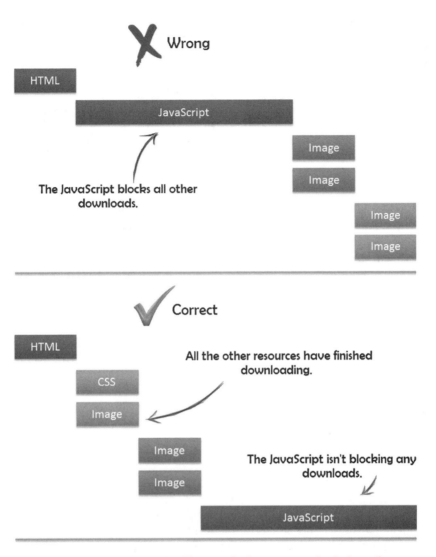

Figure 6.3   An image showing the differences in the way a page loads depending on where the JavaScript has been placed in the HTML. Note that the best place is at the bottom of the page.

JavaScript to the bottom of the page. Downloads aren't blocked, rendering takes place faster, and the user will be able to see and interact with elements on the page a lot sooner.

6.2   *How the order of styles and scripts affects rendering*

You've learned the optimal positions for CSS and JavaScript, but the order that these files are placed in an HTML page is also important. If you place them in the correct order, you're making sure the browser can render the page faster and not block the

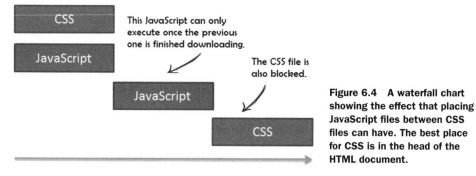

This JavaScript can only execute once the previous one is finished downloading.

The CSS file is also blocked.

Figure 6.4   A waterfall chart showing the effect that placing JavaScript files between CSS files can have. The best place for CSS is in the head of the HTML document.

download of any components while it's doing so. As mentioned earlier, the browser will delay rendering any content that follows a script tag until it's been fully downloaded. If you couple this with a browser not rendering a web page until the CSS has been parsed, the order of your style sheets and JavaScript can have a big impact on your page load times.

The next listing contains HTML with four components that need to be downloaded so the page will render. I have purposely positioned the JavaScript between the style sheets to show how this will negatively affect performance.

Listing 6.3   The order of external styles and scripts

```
<!DOCTYPE html>
<html lang="en">
<head>
<title>Sample web page</title>
<link href="Styles/bootstrap.css" rel="stylesheet" />
<script src="Scripts/jquery-1.7.2.js"></script>
<script src="Scripts/bootstrap-alert.js"></script>
<link href="Styles/bootstrap-responsive.css" rel="stylesheet" />
</head>
```

The JavaScript files are located between the two CSS files.

The waterfall chart now might look something like figure 6.4

Notice that the second JavaScript file in figure 6.4 will only execute after the first JavaScript file has been downloaded. This also affects the second CSS file because it must wait until the second JavaScript file has finished downloading before it executes. Each component is forcing the next component to wait until the preceding component is finished downloading. It's like being in a bank with only one cashier—you need to wait until the person in front of you has been assisted and finishes their transaction before you can be helped! The next listing contains updated code that shows JavaScript and CSS files in the correct order in a web page.

Listing 6.4   The correct order for external scripts and styles

```
<!DOCTYPE html>
<html lang="en">
<head>
<title>The correct order</title>
```

```
<link href="Styles/bootstrap.css" rel="stylesheet" />
<link href="Styles/bootstrap-responsive.css" rel="stylesheet" />
</head>
<body>
<script src="Scripts/jquery-1.7.2.js"></script>
<script src="Scripts/bootstrap-alert.js"></script>

</body>
</html>
```

▷— **The JavaScript files are located at the bottom of the page.**

Notice I've moved the JavaScript to the bottom of the web page, just before the close of the <body> tag. I've also kept the CSS in the document head. With the order of the external style sheets and scripts optimized, the waterfall chart for the previous listing might look something like figure 6.5.

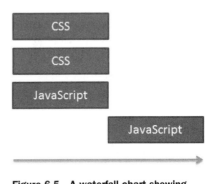
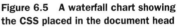

Figure 6.5 A waterfall chart showing the CSS placed in the document head

Browsers run JavaScript in a single thread, so it's understandable that while CSS and JavaScript are being parsed and executed, the browser is unable to start other downloads. But there's no reason the browser can't start downloading other resources while the CSS and JavaScript files are downloading. Now that the order of the JavaScript and CSS has been optimized, you can see in figure 6.5 that more downloads are able to occur in parallel. The two CSS files are being downloaded in parallel to the first JavaScript file and you no longer have any downloads blocking the other components on the page. Our bank now has a few more cashiers and the line isn't as long!

6.2.1 *The impact of duplicate scripts*

Duplicate scripts on your web page will not only add extraneous components for the browser to download, but will also add extra JavaScript for the browser to execute. Even if you've added HTTP caching, redundant JavaScript will still take time to parse and execute. You may be a diligent developer and think that this will never happen to you; however it can happen to anyone, especially in a team development environment. You wouldn't want all your optimization work to go to waste by having extra unnecessary JavaScript files in your application! Keep this in mind when reviewing your HTML.

6.3 *HTML5*

HTML5 is a hot topic, and web developers everywhere are beginning to embrace it. HTML5 is the latest generation of HTML, and since the previous version (HTML4), there have been syntactical changes in the structure of the markup. A few extra APIs that are accessed via JavaScript have been added to HTML5. The web is constantly evolving all around us, mobile devices such as tablets and phones are becoming more powerful and more aligned with desktop PCs. HTML5 was designed to help us progress our work in the ever-evolving world of the internet.

Some optimization techniques available in HTML5 will increase the performance and speed of your websites. In the next section, you'll learn some of these techniques. Although many of them may not improve your PageSpeed or YSlow score, they will definitely benefit your users.

In the shift between HTML4 and HTML5, the general structure of the HTML is the same, but syntactical changes reduce the number of characters you need to include on the page. Less syntax obviously contributes to the overall improved page load time. If you have less HTML in the page, the page is a lot lighter and the user is able to download the request faster.

In previous versions of HTML you would specify the document type at the top of the page like so:

```
<!DOCTYPE html PUBLIC "-//W3C//DTD XHTML 1.0 Strict//EN"
"http://www.w3.org/TR/xhtml1/DTD/xhtml1-strict.dtd">
```

HTML5 now allows you to set the document type in the following manner:

```
<!DOCTYPE html>
```

The same applies when you specify the encoding of your document. Older versions of HTML would be similar to the following:

```
<meta http-equiv="content-type" content="text/html; charset=utf-8">
```

HTML5 now allows you to specify it like so:

```
<meta charset="utf-8">
```

These changes might not seem like much, but you're already starting to remove extraneous characters and reduce the overall page weights in your website. Another syntactical change introduced with HTML5 is the ability to exclude type attributes when you're referencing resources on your web page. For example, you might have referenced a JavaScript file like this in an older version of HTML:

```
<script type="text/javascript" src="filename">
```

However, you no longer need to specify the script type.

```
<script src="filename">
```

This can be applied to style sheets and, in fact, all MIME types in your web page. You can simply exclude the MIME types in the type attribute. Each step toward character removal means that you're reducing the size of the HTML page to be loaded.

6.4   *A note on HTML5 browser support*

Although HTML5 is starting to gain popularity and exposure across the internet, it's still in its infancy in terms of overall adoption. You've covered a handful of great HTML5 techniques that can really improve your application's performance, but you

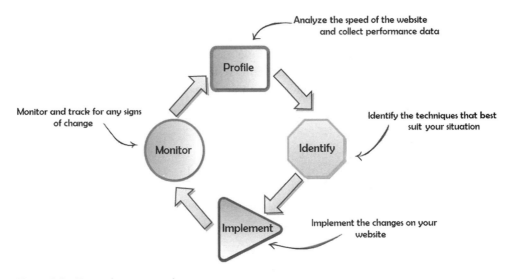

Figure 6.6 The performance cycle

should always keep in mind that a lot of browsers don't yet support some of these great HTML5 features.

With the right fallbacks in place, there is no reason why you can't start using HTML5 today.

Modernizr (download at http://modernizr.com/) is a JavaScript library that detects HTML5 and CSS3 features in a user's browser. It's great if you need to quickly and easily determine the capabilities of a user's browser, which then allows you to serve them the appropriate content.

Chapter 1 covered the performance cycle and the important role it plays when you're making changes on your website. While you're progressing through this chapter, keep the stages of the performance cycle (figure 6.6; repeated from chapter 1) and where you currently stand in mind. After applying any HTML5 updates to a website, it's important to monitor any performance changes and monitor how they affect your users. As a developer, think about your users instead of simply adding HTML5 features. What do your analytics statistics look like? How many of your users are using updated browsers? How long does your JavaScript take to load? These are all important questions to ask yourself.

6.4.1 *HTML5 asynchronous JavaScript*

At the beginning of the chapter you learned about the impact JavaScript has on web page loading times. JavaScript will block any other downloads on a page, and in some instances prevent the page from progressively rendering. Many a time you will see a blank page while a large JavaScript file is being downloaded and parsed, and it's because it's blocking the DOM. However, the clever folks, at the W3C thought of a way to get around this.

Enter async, an attribute of the script tag, introduced in the HTML5 draft. This handy little attribute allows you to download JavaScript and execute it asynchronously without blocking the rendering of elements below it. Think of it as the browser's ability to execute the code independently of anything else that's happening on the page. The best part is it doesn't block anything else. You simply need to include async in the script tag:

```
<script async src="filename"></script>
```

In theory, if you have two scripts in a web page and you're using async, these two scripts can run at the same time and in parallel.

Another useful tag attribute is defer. It can be used in conjunction with async and has been supported in browsers for a while now. In order to use it, add the attribute to the script tag:

```
<script defer src="filename"></script>
```

The defer attribute is similar to async in most ways. The difference is when each script is executed. Each async script executes after it has finished downloading, which means it is not executed in the order in which it occurs in the page. The defer scripts are guaranteed to be executed in the order in which they occur in the page. The following listing shows an example of these tags being used in a web page.

Listing 6.5   An example of asynchronous JavaScript in action

```
<!DOCTYPE html>
<html lang="en">
<head>
<title>Async JavaScript</title>
<link href="Styles/Site.css" rel="stylesheet" />
    </head>
    <body>
        <img src="Images/Image1.png" >
        <img src="Images/Image2.png" >
        <img src="Images/Image3.png" >
        <img src="Images/Image4.png" >

        <script async src="Scripts/tracking.js"></script>
    </body>
    </html>
```

The async attribute added to the JavaScript tag

The async attribute is included in the JavaScript tag. Figure 6.7 shows a waterfall chart for a web page, like that in the previous listing, which has script tags decorated with the async attribute. Notice that the JavaScript will still get executed in any order that the browser sees fit, even if the JavaScript appears at the bottom of the page. The async attribute allows the browser to parse the HTML and decide when and how to download and execute the JavaScript. This has also occurred independently of the other downloads on the page.

There are still some things you'll need to take into account when you're using async and defer. The scripts aren't guaranteed to run in the order they appear in

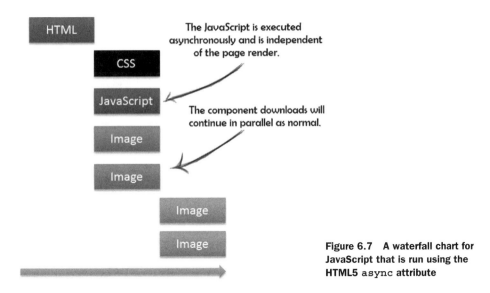

Figure 6.7   A waterfall chart for JavaScript that is run using the HTML5 `async` attribute

the document, which is their default behavior when `async` isn't present. You'll need to exercise caution when using these two attributes because they might lead to code dependency issues. For instance, if you use jQuery or any other JavaScript library on your web page that's used by other scripts on the same page, you might find that the script that's dependent on the library is run first. This can cause the scripts to fail. Figure 6.8 represents a typical JavaScript error you might come across in this situation.

Depending on your HTML, the usage of `async` or `defer` can bring a boost to the JavaScript performance of a web page. It can get a little tricky when the JavaScript on the web page has dependencies, so keep that in mind.

6.4.2   HTML5 Web Workers

JavaScript runs in a single-threaded environment, so multiple scripts can't run at the same time. It also means expensive, long-running tasks may block UI rendering. It would be a whole lot easier if you could write JavaScript asynchronous tasks that are both fire-and-forget and won't block the UI of a web page.

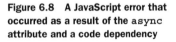

Figure 6.8   A JavaScript error that occurred as a result of the `async` attribute and a code dependency

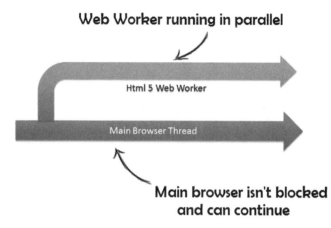

Web Worker running in parallel

Html 5 Web Worker

Main Browser Thread

Main browser isn't blocked and can continue

Figure 6.9   Web Workers are able to run in parallel to the main browser thread.

Fortunately, there is an API that allows you to run scripts in the background, isolated from the web page. This API is known as Web Workers. Workers use thread-like messaging and they are perfect for keeping your UI fresh, snappy, and responsive. What is the difference between simply decorating your script tag with the `async` attribute and using HTML5 Web Workers? HTML5 Web Workers actually run in a thread that is owned by the browser. I like to think of HTML5 Web Workers as `Thread` or `ThreadPool` classes from .NET's System.Threading namespace for the front end.

Thankfully, HTML5 Web Workers allow you to run tasks in parallel, and this makes full use of multiprocessor computers. Figure 6.9 illustrates how HTML5 Web Workers run in parallel to the UI thread, allowing the main browser to continue as normal, not blocked by the JavaScript.

Web Workers are perfect for fire-and-forget tasks. If you have a long-running task that you want to run in the background without affecting the main page, using a Web Worker would be ideal.

Using Web Workers can also be useful if you need to make sure a snippet of script executes even if the user navigates away from the web page. For example, if a user on your site navigates to another web page, you might find that a long-running script can't finish executing and you could lose your JavaScript objects. If you use a Web Worker, script execution happens in another thread, so you can guarantee that it will execute properly.

Next you're going to implement a basic, long-running AJAX example in the Surf Store application. As you progress through this example, remember that this Web Workers exercise is merely intended to give you a better understanding of Web Workers. The example you're using is not a real-world scenario, and you'll need to think about how to apply this to your application first!

6.4.3   *Browser support for HTML5 Web Workers*

You're about to run code samples in both MVC and Web Forms. Surprisingly, there is a decent amount of support for Web Workers, but some of the major browsers (including older versions of Internet Explorer) are still playing a bit of catch-up. Firefox, Chrome, Safari, Opera, and Internet Explorer 10 all offer support for Web Workers. For more information, caniuse.com is a useful website for determining which browsers support Web Workers and any other HTML5 features. If the browser you're targeting doesn't yet fully support Web Workers, you could fall back to using traditional methods for executing long-running scripts.

6.4.4 HTML5 Web Workers in an ASP.NET MVC application

Remember that the original sample code for each application can be downloaded at https://github.com/deanhume/FastASPNetWebsites. Once it is in place, open the MVC project in the chapter 6 source code under the folder HTML5 Web Workers. In your Solution Explorer, navigate to the Layout View. Add the code from this listing.

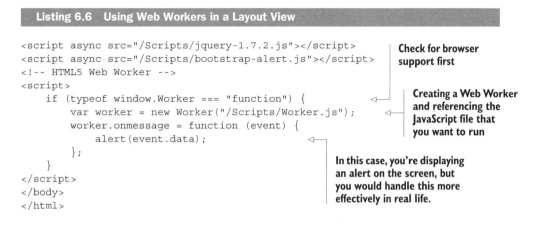

Listing 6.6 Using Web Workers in a Layout View

```
<script async src="/Scripts/jquery-1.7.2.js"></script>          Check for browser
<script async src="/Scripts/bootstrap-alert.js"></script>       support first
<!-- HTML5 Web Worker -->
<script>
    if (typeof window.Worker === "function") {                  Creating a Web Worker
        var worker = new Worker("/Scripts/Worker.js");           and referencing the
        worker.onmessage = function (event) {                    JavaScript file that
            alert(event.data);                                   you want to run
        };
    }                                     In this case, you're displaying
</script>                                 an alert on the screen, but
</body>                                   you would handle this more
</html>                                   effectively in real life.
```

You added the JavaScript just before the closing `<body>` tag, because this code will run asynchronously but you don't want to block other component downloads on the page.

Remember that the order of scripts and styles can affect page rendering! Next, add a new JavaScript file called Worker.js to your Scripts folder in the project. You'll use this Worker.js file to create the code the HTML5 Web Worker will execute. Figure 6.10 shows the location of the newly created Worker.js file in the Surf Store application for this chapter.

Inside the JavaScript file (Worker.js), add the code in the following listing.

Figure 6.10 Adding a new JavaScript file to the Scripts folder in an ASP.NET MVC application

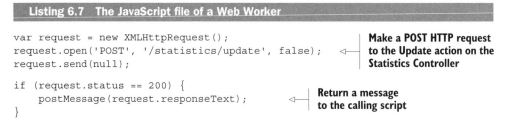

Listing 6.7   The JavaScript file of a Web Worker

```
var request = new XMLHttpRequest();
request.open('POST', '/statistics/update', false);
request.send(null);

if (request.status == 200) {
    postMessage(request.responseText);
}
```

Make a POST HTTP request to the Update action on the Statistics Controller

Return a message to the calling script

The Worker.js file contains code that will make an AJAX request to a controller in the MVC application. You're going to update a set of statistics on the server with this code and it will return a message to the main calling script once the code has completed. You're not passing any parameters in this example, but these could just as easily be added onto the request. Web Workers use a method called `postMessage` to return a result to the thread that called it. Whatever you return in this `postMessage` will be returned to the original thread. Next, you'll need to add the controller that's going to simulate intensive server-side code.

Add this new controller to the application and call it `StatisticsController`. This controller will contain the code that will execute and update the statistics on the server. The code in listing 6.8 is simple, but it's used to simulate what could happen if the server needed to perform intensive calculations or long-running database calls. In the case of the code in the example listing, it's updating the statistics for the website in the database which is an expensive call if done regularly. If you fire up the application, you'll notice that you can continue using the web page and nothing has blocked the UI. You'll receive an alert message once the operation that was running in the background has completed.

Listing 6.8   The JavaScript file of a Web Worker

```
public ActionResult Update()
{
    // This takes 5 seconds to execute
    Thread.Sleep();

    return Json("Success", JsonRequestBehavior.AllowGet);
}
```

The code is making the application wait in order to simulate a long-running process.

Return a success message to the Worker.js script

In figure 6.11, the image of the Network tab on the developer tools shows us a similar result.

In the Network tab, Worker.js is shown to take only 48 milliseconds. However, it actually took 5 seconds. It only took 48 milliseconds for the browser to parse the initial JavaScript and hand it off to run in parallel. The Web Worker allowed it to run in the background and it had no effect on the page's UI. Through the clever use of JavaScript threads this brilliant HTML5 feature has drastically sped up the load time and responsiveness of the web page.

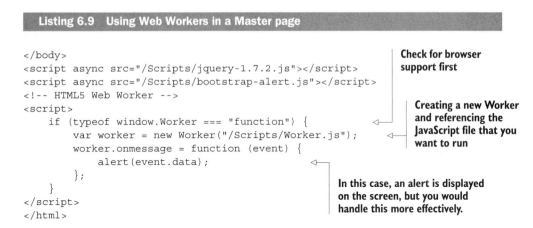

Figure 6.11 The Web Worker in the Network tab in an ASP.NET MVC application

6.4.5 Web Workers in an ASP.NET Web Forms application

Adding HTML5 Web Workers to your ASP.NET Web Forms application is easy. In fact, adding Web Workers to even the most simple HTML page can be done in no time. In this example, you're going to see how a Web Worker makes a call to an AJAX-enabled WCF service.

First, open the Web Forms project in the chapter 6 source code under the folder HTML5 Web Workers. In your Solution Explorer, navigate to the Site.Master page. Add the code in this listing outside of the <body> tag.

Listing 6.9 Using Web Workers in a Master page

```
</body>
<script async src="/Scripts/jquery-1.7.2.js"></script>          Check for browser
<script async src="/Scripts/bootstrap-alert.js"></script>       support first
<!-- HTML5 Web Worker -->
<script>                                                         Creating a new Worker
    if (typeof window.Worker === "function") {          ◁        and referencing the
        var worker = new Worker("/Scripts/Worker.js");  ◁        JavaScript file that you
        worker.onmessage = function (event) {                    want to run
            alert(event.data);                          ◁
        };
    }                                                   In this case, an alert is displayed
}                                                       on the screen, but you would
</script>                                               handle this more effectively.
</html>
```

We added the JavaScript outside of the <body> tag because even though this code will run asynchronously, we still don't want to block other component downloads on the page. Remember that the order of scripts and styles can affect the page rendering! Next, add a new JavaScript file called Worker.js to your Scripts folder in the project. Figure 6.12 shows where the newly created Worker.js file is located in the Surf Store application.

Inside the JavaScript file, add the following code:

Listing 6.10   The JavaScript file of a Web Worker

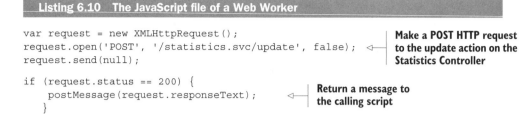

```
var request = new XMLHttpRequest();
request.open('POST', '/statistics.svc/update', false);   ⊲─┤  Make a POST HTTP request
request.send(null);                                           to the update action on the
                                                              Statistics Controller
if (request.status == 200) {
    postMessage(request.responseText);      ⊲─┤  Return a message to
    }                                            the calling script
```

The Worker.js file contains code that is going to make a request to an AJAX-enabled WCF service in the Web Forms application. Once it's completed, it will return a message to the main calling script. In this example, you're not passing any parameters through, but these could easily be added onto the request. Web Workers use `postMessage` to return a result to the calling thread. Whatever you return in this `postMessage` will be returned to the original thread. Next, you need to add the AJAX-enabled WCF service that is going to simulate long-running server-side code.

Add this new AJAX-enabled WCF service, shown in the following listing, to the application and call it `Statistics`. This WCF service will contain the code that will execute and update the statistics on the server.

Figure 6.12   Adding a new JavaScript file to the Scripts folder in an ASP.NET Web Forms application

Listing 6.11   The server-side code of an AJAX-enabled WCF service

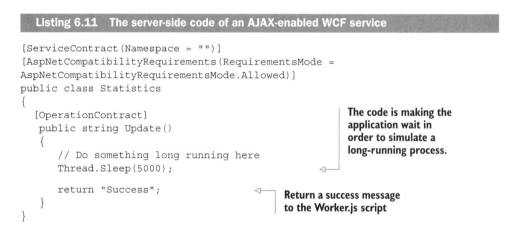

```
[ServiceContract(Namespace = "")]
[AspNetCompatibilityRequirements(RequirementsMode =
AspNetCompatibilityRequirementsMode.Allowed)]
public class Statistics
{
    [OperationContract]
    public string Update()                        The code is making the
    {                                             application wait in
        // Do something long running here         order to simulate a
        Thread.Sleep(5000);              ⊲─┤      long-running process.

        return "Success";      ⊲─┤  Return a success message
    }                               to the Worker.js script
}
```

This code is simple, but it is used to simulate what could happen if the server needed to perform intensive calculations or long-running database calls. If you fire up the application, you'll notice that you can continue using the web page and nothing has blocked the UI. You'll receive an alert message once the operation that was running in the background has completed. The Network tab in browser developer tools (figure 6.13) shows us a similar result.

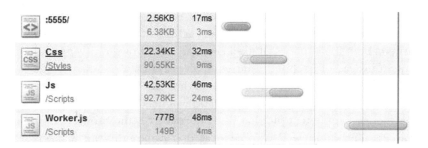

Figure 6.13   The Web Worker being downloaded and executed in an ASP.NET Web Forms application

In the Network tab, the Worker.js is shown to take only 48 milliseconds. However, it actually took 5 seconds. This is because it took only 48 milliseconds for the browser to parse the JavaScript and pass it off to run in parallel. The Web Worker allowed it to run in the background and had no effect on the page's UI. Through the clever use of JavaScript threads this brilliant HTML5 feature has drastically sped up the load time and responsiveness of the web page.

6.5   *HTML5 application cache*

Another great feature introduced in HTML5 is the application cache which allows you to run your web application offline. If the application cache is utilized properly, you won't need a network connection to browse the pages in a website. This feature may not be applicable to every application that you write, but you can harness it to improve the speed and load times of certain pages in a web application. This technique does seem like a great concept—but how does it actually help you improve the speed of an application? The user could access all the resources that they need from the application cache instead of the server and, in turn, the page would load a lot faster.

A web browser that uses the HTML5 application cache to implement offline applications will read a list of URLs from the manifest file, download the resources, cache them locally, and automatically keep the local copies up-to-date as they change. Figure 6.14 represents the flow of events that take place in the HTML5 application cache.

The HTML5 application cache enables a website to function without a network connection, and it can be extremely useful when a user on a mobile connection suddenly loses signal. This feature feels like something you should have been able to do

Figure 6.14   The HTML5 application cache workflow

for years with web pages, and now it's finally been implemented as part of HTML5. Another advantage of using the application cache is it acts like the HTTP caching that you learned about in chapter 4. If used correctly, the browser only needs to download new content instead of fetching resources it already has.

Using the HTML5 application cache in an ASP.NET application is an easy process. Each time you use the application cache, you will need to reference a cache manifest file. This file is a simple text file that lists the resources the browser should cache for offline access. The manifest file can be located anywhere on your web server and contains a list of the things you'll want to store in the application cache.

In order to know which files to cache, the HTML5 application cache will look inside the manifest file. This file will contain a simple list of the files that you want to cache. A typical manifest may look similar to the output in this listing.

Listing 6.12 A typical cache manifest file

```
CACHE MANIFEST
index.html
stylesheet.css
images/logo.png
scripts/main.js
```

You could always link to a static manifest file on your server, but I quite like to use the power of ASP.NET to return a dynamic manifest file. A dynamic file gives you much more control over the individual files you want to cache, and also allows for tighter control of updating the cache. You're going to look at an example in both ASP.NET Web Forms and ASP.NET MVC that easily allows you to harness the power of this great HTML5 feature. By using a dynamic manifest file, the browser will continue to use the cached version of the resources until the manifest file has changed or been updated.

A manifest file is made up of three sections: CACHE, NETWORK, and FALLBACK. Each section has a specific purpose:

- *CACHE*—This section contains the list of files to cache. Files listed in this section will be explicitly cached after they're downloaded for the first time.
- *NETWORK*—Files listed in this section require a connection to the server. Resources in this section are never cached and are not available offline.
- *FALLBACK*—This section contains a list of files that can act as a fallback if a user has no connection or the file is inaccessible.

You're about to look at examples in both ASP.NET MVC and ASP.NET Web Forms that will give you a better idea of how the HTML5 application cache works.

6.5.1 *HTML5 application cache considerations*

Remember that any pages you add to the manifest attribute will be cached in the browser: this includes the page itself! You can't cache the resources and not the page because it isn't designed to work that way. Think of the HTML5 application cache as extreme HTTP caching. The disadvantage of using the application cache is it doesn't play well with server-side dynamic pages. If you keep your own website in mind, the pages you would add to the application cache would normally be the static pages or pages that don't change very often. If you add the manifest attribute to your Master Page or Layout View, you'll cache your entire application and won't notice any changes when you refresh. Consider adding this to pages that aren't updated dynamically.

> **NOTE** Using the HTML5 application cache in your projects can make debugging your application a nightmare, so if you're reloading your page and you're only seeing the cached version, you'll need to make a change to the manifest file in order for the browser to fetch the new version. Alternatively, you'll need to clear the application cache for the site. Check your browser for the particular settings in order to clear the application cache.

6.5.2 *HTML5 application cache in an ASP.NET MVC application*

Now you're going to run through the Surf Store application and update it to use the HTML5 application cache. This will cache certain components on a page within the user's browser and enable dramatically faster load times. You're going to use the power of ASP.NET and make the Application Manifest file dynamic so you have more control over the items that you're caching.

To enable the application cache you'll need to include the `manifest` attribute on the HTML tag on the view that you wish to add to the application cache. Because the entire HTML page will be cached itself, you're going to use pages that don't change often, such as the About or Contact page. You're going to use an MVC Controller to dynamically generate the manifest file and check the contents of the files that are being referenced. Update the Contact view in the project to reflect the code in the following listing.

Listing 6.13 Referencing the manifest file

```
@{
    ViewBag.Title = "Contact";
}

<!DOCTYPE html>
<html lang="en" manifest="/AppCache">       ⟵  Reference to the AppCache controller
<head>                                          will also point to a route in your
    <meta charset="utf-8">                      application that will contain the
    <title>Surf Store Application</title>       dynamic manifest file.
    <link rel="shortcut icon"
       ➥ href="@Url.Content("~/Content/Images/favicon.ico")" />
    <meta name="viewport" content="width=device-width, initial-scale=1.0">
    <meta name="description" content="">
    <meta name="author" content="">
    <link href="@Url.Content("~/Content/Css/bootstrap.css")"
       ➥ rel="stylesheet"/>
<link href="@Url.Content("~/Content/Css/bootstrap-responsive.css")"
       ➥ rel="stylesheet"/>
```

In the listing you've updated the HTML tag to reference the MVC Controller. You'll use this controller to dynamically generate the references to the files that you're going to store in the browser. Now you'll create your dynamic manifest page. First, add a new controller and call it `AppCacheController`. Then add a new method on your controller called `Index`, so the MVC route will map to /AppCache. Notice in the following listing how the MVC route matches up to the manifest link that you supplied on the HTML tag.

Listing 6.14   The `AppCacheController`

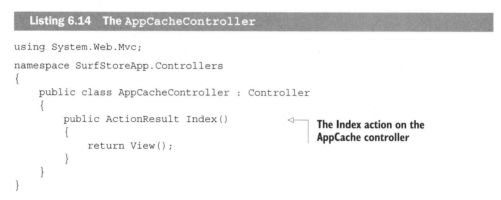

```
using System.Web.Mvc;

namespace SurfStoreApp.Controllers
{
    public class AppCacheController : Controller
    {
        public ActionResult Index()          ◁———  The Index action on the
        {                                           AppCache controller
            return View();
        }
    }
}
```

Next, add a view for that `ActionResult`. This view will contain the contents of the manifest file, shown next.

Listing 6.15   The dynamic manifest file

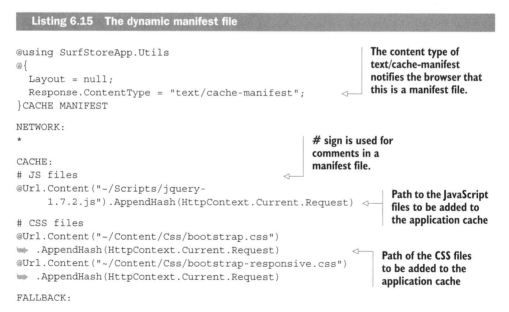

```
@using SurfStoreApp.Utils                           The content type of
@{                                                  text/cache-manifest
  Layout = null;                                    notifies the browser that
  Response.ContentType = "text/cache-manifest";  ◁— this is a manifest file.
}CACHE MANIFEST

NETWORK:
*                                           # sign is used for
                                            comments in a
CACHE:                                      manifest file.
# JS files                               ◁—
@Url.Content("~/Scripts/jquery-
    1.7.2.js").AppendHash(HttpContext.Current.Request)  ◁—  Path to the JavaScript
                                                             files to be added to
# CSS files                                                  the application cache
@Url.Content("~/Content/Css/bootstrap.css")
➥ .AppendHash(HttpContext.Current.Request)           ◁—
@Url.Content("~/Content/Css/bootstrap-responsive.css")     Path of the CSS files
➥ .AppendHash(HttpContext.Current.Request)                to be added to the
                                                            application cache
FALLBACK:
```

In chapter 5 you learned about file revving, a technique that appends a query string to the end of a filename to make sure a fresh version is retrieved every time a file changes. You're going to apply the same technique to the manifest file, because you only want it to be updated when the contents of the referenced files change.

Figure 6.15   The browser creating an application cache and downloading the contents in an ASP.NET MVC application

In the previous code you'll notice a method called AppendHash() on the end of the filenames. This method will read the contents of the file referenced and only change the hash that's appended if the contents of the file change. This makes the application cache entirely dynamic because there's no need to update your manifest file every time a resource (CSS, JavaScript, and so on) file changes. This forces the browser to request a new version of the file.

Using the developer tools in a browser is the best way to inspect the application cache. If you open the web page in Google Chrome and navigate to the Console tab in the developer tools, you'll notice something similar to figure 6.15.

In figure 6.15 the browser is downloading the items referenced in the manifest file you created. You can also use the Chrome developer tools to inspect the exact items that have been stored in the application cache (figure 6.16).

By navigating to the Resources tab and choosing Application Cache, you'll be able to inspect the files that have been added to the application cache. In figure 6.16 you will also notice that a hash string has been appended to the end of the filenames. This means AppendHash is working correctly, and if the contents of the static files were to change, the application cache would fetch the updated versions based on the new hash key.

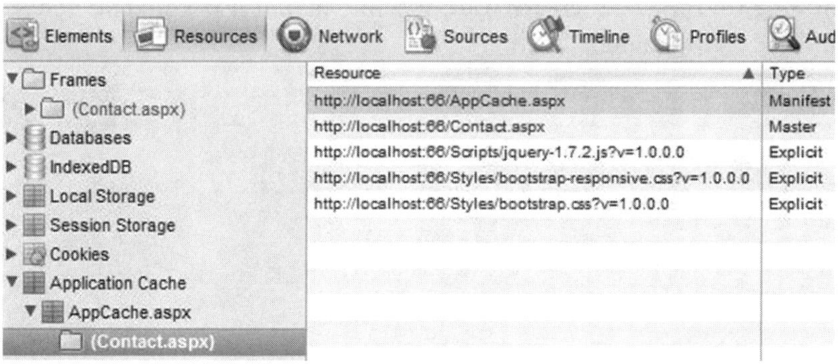

Figure 6.16   The resources stored in the application cache in an ASP.NET MVC application

Every time a user who's had an application cache created in their browser reloads the page and requests the same resources, it will be fetched from the browser's cache and never hit the server. Now the web page can be accessed while they're offline.

6.5.3 *HTML5 application cache in an ASP.NET Web Forms application*

Using the Surf Store application, you can easily update the code to use the HTML5 application cache. You're going to use the power of ASP.NET Web Forms and make the application manifest file dynamic so you have more control over the items you're caching. In order to enable the application cache, you need to include the `manifest` attribute on the HTML tag on the page you wish to add to the application cache. Because the entire HTML page will get cached, you're going to use pages that don't change often, such as the About or Contact page. In order to dynamically generate a manifest file, you're going to use an ASP.NET Web Forms page. Open the Contact view in the project to reflect the code in the following listing.

Listing 6.16   Referencing the manifest file

```
<%@ Page Title="" Language="C#" AutoEventWireup="true"
    CodeBehind="Contact.aspx.cs" Inherits="SurfStoreApp.Contact" %>

<!DOCTYPE html>
<html lang="en" manifest="AppCache.aspx">        A reference to the
<head>                                            AppCache controller
        <meta charset="utf-8">
        <title>Surf Store Application</title>
        <link rel="shortcut icon" href="Images/favicon.ico" />
        <meta name="viewport" content="width=device-width,
          ➥ initial-scale=1.0">
        <meta name="description" content="">
        <meta name="author" content="">
        <link href="Styles/bootstrap.css" rel="stylesheet" />
        <link href="Styles/bootstrap-responsive.css" rel="stylesheet" />
```

You've updated the HTML tag to reference a Web Forms web page. You'll use this ASPX web page to dynamically generate the references to the files that you're going to store in the browser. Next, create your dynamic manifest page. First, add a new web page and call it AppCache.

Listing 6.17   The dynamic manifest file

```
<%@ Page Language="C#" AutoEventWireup="true"
  ➥ CodeBehind="AppCache.aspx.cs" Inherits="SurfStoreApp.AppCache" %>
<%@ Import Namespace="SurfStoreApp.Utils" %>
<% HttpContext.Current
  ➥ .Response.ContentType = "text/cache-manifest"; %>CACHE MANIFEST

NETWORK:
*

CACHE:
# JS files
<%= "Scripts/jquery-1.7.2.js".AppendHash(Request) %>
```

Content type of text/manifest notifies the browser that this is a manifest file.

sign is used for comments.

Path to the JavaScript files that are to be added to the application cache

```
# CSS files
<%= "Styles/bootstrap.css".AppendHash(Request)  %>
<%= "Styles/bootstrap-responsive.css".AppendHash(Request)  %>
FALLBACK:
```

◁── **Path of the CSS files that are to be added to the application cache**

In chapter 5 you learned about file revving, which appends a query string to the end of a filename to ensure a fresh version of a file is retrieved every time a file changes. You're going to apply the same technique to the manifest file, because you only want it to get updated when the contents of the referenced files change.

In the previous code you'll notice there is a method called AppendHash() on the end of the filenames. This method will read the contents of the file referenced and only change the hash that's appended if the contents of the file change. This makes the application cache entirely dynamic because there's no need to update your manifest file every time a resource (CSS, JavaScript, and so on) file has changed. This will force the browser to request a new version of the file.

Using the developer tools in a browser is the best way to inspect the application cache of your Web Forms application. If you open the web page in Google Chrome, you will notice something similar to figure 6.17.

In figure 6.17, the browser is downloading the items that are referenced in the manifest file that you created. If you refresh the page, you'll see the browser will simply retrieve the files it needs from the application cache.

Using the HTML5 application cache in your ASP.NET Web Forms application can be an effective way of improving the load time of your web pages.

6.5.4 Application cache support

By adding these changes to your application you're ensuring the user's browser will no longer retrieve the files from your server, but will instead fetch them from its own cache (figure 6.18). This can be a good thing and a dangerous thing. Use the HTML5 application cache wisely! It's important to remember that using the HTML5 application cache might not suit your situation, depending on the purpose of your web application. If you have a dynamic website that relies on constantly providing your users with fresh content, this might not be the best solution for you. Instead, only use it on pages that don't change often or pages that won't be affected by this level of caching.

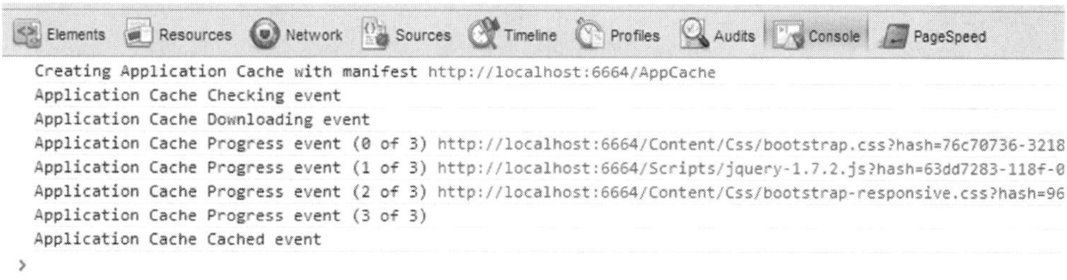

```
Elements    Resources    Network    Sources    Timeline    Profiles    Audits    Console    PageSpeed

 Creating Application Cache with manifest http://localhost:6664/AppCache
 Application Cache Checking event
 Application Cache Downloading event
 Application Cache Progress event (0 of 3) http://localhost:6664/Content/Css/bootstrap.css?hash=76c70736-3218
 Application Cache Progress event (1 of 3) http://localhost:6664/Scripts/jquery-1.7.2.js?hash=63dd7283-118f-0
 Application Cache Progress event (2 of 3) http://localhost:6664/Content/Css/bootstrap-responsive.css?hash=96
 Application Cache Progress event (3 of 3)
 Application Cache Cached event
 >
```

Figure 6.17 The browser creating an application cache and downloading the contents in an ASP.NET Web Forms application

Document was loaded from Application Cache with manifest http://localhost:66/A
Application Cache Checking event
Application Cache NoUpdate event

**Figure 6.18   The events that take place in a browser when an application cache
is requested in an ASP.NET Web Forms application**

6.6   *Summary*

There are some important best practices that should be applied to your HTML in
order to achieve the best load times from your web pages. This chapter answered a few
vital questions about how resources should be placed in a web page's HTML, and
you've covered some pretty cool HTML5 features. When used correctly, HTML5 can be
harnessed to improve your web page's performance. HTML5 doesn't require as many
HTML attributes in order for the browser to interpret and display its resources, so you
can use fewer characters in your web page's HTML. That's great because fewer characters equal faster download times.

Another great feature of HTML5 is Web Workers. You can use them to execute long-
running JavaScript code in a separate thread of your browser. This feature is great if you
need to pass large amounts of data to the server side or if you need to perform intensive
number crunching on the client. The HTML5 application cache can also bring performance benefits to your website. It is designed to allow you to run your web application
offline and can be harnessed to improve your application's load time.

In the next chapter, we're going to take a look at image optimizations and how you
can squeeze those precious bytes out of your images to substantially speed up your
page load times.

Image optimization 7

This chapter covers

- The importance of image optimization
- Online and command line image optimization tools
- Automatic data URIs

As the old saying goes, "A picture is worth a thousand words." Most websites today rely heavily on images to enhance their visual look and feel, so it isn't surprising to learn that images often make up the bulk of a web page. Every byte counts in performance optimization and it's important to optimize these images as much as possible.

In this chapter you're going to learn about techniques you can apply to your website's images that will reduce their file size and reduce the overall weight of your web pages. Modern image optimization techniques are proven to reduce image size by stripping unnecessary data from the file, thus reducing the file size without affecting image quality. The images on your website will look exactly the same but will be significantly lighter and quicker to download. You will learn how to use online and command line image optimization tools that will make a big difference to the size of your web pages. In this chapter, you will also discover data URIs and how they can be used with images in order to reduce the number of HTTP requests that a web page makes.

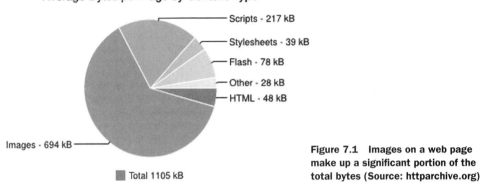

Figure 7.1 Images on a web page make up a significant portion of the total bytes (Source: httparchive.org)

7.1   What's the big deal with image optimization?

Images are a huge part of the internet today. Whether your website is a glossy e-commerce site, a magazine website, or a small blog, you will have made use of images at some point. Using images on your website can add and enhance the design, but they may add unnecessary bytes depending on the size and quality of the images. As you can see in figure 7.1, if you break down the components of the average website, you'll find the bulk of the bytes come from the images.

The chart in figure 7.1, produced by httparchive.org and used with permission, shows the average number of bytes per content type on web pages. You can see that the images on an average web page make up a large portion of the overall bytes. In this case, this is almost 63%! Remember that even if you make big gains and reduce the size of scripts, styles, and HTML in a web page, the largest component may be the images. The easiest way to improve page performance, without removing any features, is to optimize the images. You don't want to waste all the optimization work you've done thus far by including bloated images in your website. Leading up to this chapter, you've focused your optimization efforts on techniques such as compression, HTTP caching, minifying and bundling, and HTML optimization. But there's been no direct emphasis on images as of yet. In chapter 3, you learned that compression is highly effective for removing extra bytes in a web page, but it can't be applied to images because they're already compressed.

If images are already compressed, how do you go about reducing the size of the files? Well, there are a few techniques you're going to cover in this chapter that will help you reduce the size of your image files significantly.

7.2   Online image optimization tools

I know that whenever I display images on a web page, I like to ensure that the image quality and clarity are as high as possible. Modern mobile phones, tablets, and computer screens are moving toward ultrahigh resolution screens that are capable of showing images at their best. The last thing you want to do is let image quality suffer

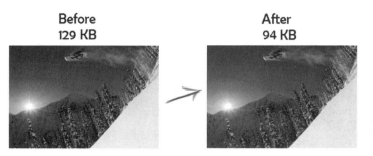

Before
129 KB

After
94 KB

Figure 7.2   Image quality isn't affected by lossless optimization.

when you reduce the size of an image. If you work in an organization with UI or graphic designers, they won't be pleased with you if they find out their images have lost quality and become pixelated! Fortunately there are free tools available that optimize images without changing their look or visual quality. This is known as *lossless optimization*, and it ensures that the quality of the image will not degrade.

There's visually no difference between the images in figure 7.2. The file size has been reduced, but the quality hasn't changed during the optimization process. Although 35 KB is only a small savings, every file size reduction you make to the images on your web page means the overall page weight will begin to improve. Now I'm going to describe some of those free tools you can use to optimize and reduce the file size of your images. These are just a few of the tools that are available on the internet, so look for the tool that best suits your needs.

7.2.1   *Smush.it*

Smush.it is my favorite image optimization tool by far. It's an online tool built by the team at Yahoo!, and is freely available at http://www.smushit.com/ysmush.it/. The tool is easy to use. You simply choose the files you wish to optimize and upload them to the smush.it website. Once optimization is complete, the tool will finish running and allow you to download the optimized images. The site also shows you the total file savings you'll gain with all the images that you uploaded.

Smush.it will take most image formats (JPG, JPEG, PNG, and GIF) and process them for you. You're going to work with the images in the Surf Store application later in the chapter so you can use the tool and see how effective it is at file optimization. Figure 7.3 shows the results from processing some image files with Smush.it, allowing you to compare your original file sizes to the optimized file sizes.

As you can see, you managed to cut 143.07 KB from the images—this is a significant chunk of data! All unnecessary metadata was stripped from the files without changing or otherwise affecting the quality of the images.

7.2.2   *Kraken*

Another freely available online image optimization tool is Kraken. Available at http://kraken.io/, this tool is similar to Yahoo! Smush.it and offers support for all major image formats.

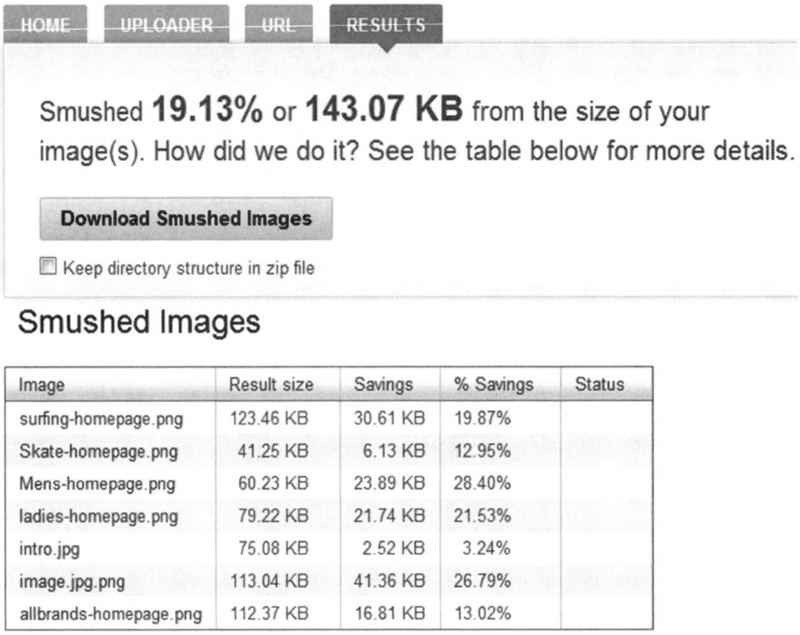

Figure 7.3   **The file savings gained by using the Yahoo! Smush.it tool**

The site offers plugins for both Firefox and Chrome that allow you to optimize all the images on a web page. This tool is definitely worth considering.

7.3   *Command line image optimization tools*

Using a manual tool such as Smush.it requires a lot of human intervention, and depending on the frequency of your website updates, it may not always be the best option. But there are a few command line tools you can use to automate the image optimization process.

The one downside to using command line tools is each tool is aimed at a specific image format. Therefore you'll need to run a different tool for each image format you work with. If done correctly, this can be achieved easily and integrated into your build or continuous integration process, which means the image optimization process becomes totally automated.

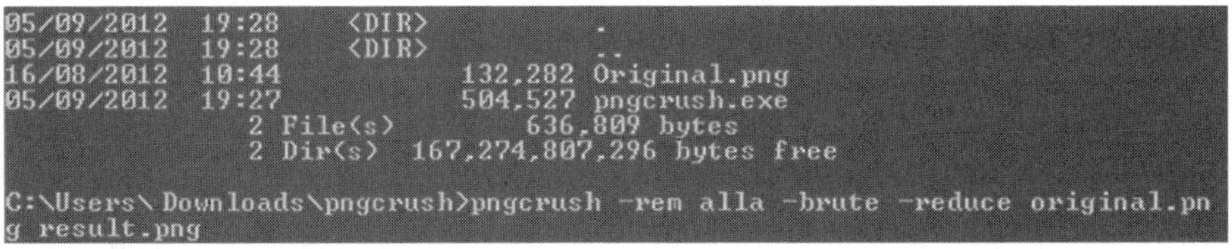

Figure 7.4   **The command line settings for Pngcrush**

7.3.1 Pngcrush

Pngcrush is a free image optimizer for PNG images. This image format is common on the web today, and all modern browsers support it. Pngcrush is available at http://pmt.sourceforge.NET/pngcrush/. Once you've downloaded the tool, simply fire up your command line in Windows and use the syntax in figure 7.4.

I've added a test image called original.png to the same directory as Pngcrush.exe. If you break this command line down, the key details are:

- *original.png*—The name of the source PNG image you're optimizing.
- *result.png*—The destination PNG file that's created after the image has been optimized.

Once the tool has finished running, you'll have a new file in the same folder called result.png. Depending on the contents and make-up of the image, the overall file size should be significantly reduced. Unfortunately, this tool is only for PNG format files and you'll need to run other tools to process other image file formats.

7.3.2 Jpegtran

A great tool that's free and easy to use in a command line is Jpegtran. It can be run against the JPEG format and the command line setup is pretty similar to Pngcrush. To download the tool, visit http://jpegclub.org/jpegtran/. The site seems a little basic, but the tool works well and is efficient as a command line image optimizer for JPEGs.

Once you've downloaded the tool, fire up your command line in Windows. The syntax in figure 7.5 will process an image with the Jpegtran tool.

I've added a test image called original.jpg to the same directory as jpegtran.exe. If you break this command line down, the key details are:

- *original.jpg*—The name of the source jpg that you're optimizing.
- *result.jpg*—The destination JPEG file that's created after the image has been optimized.

You'll notice that the command line and processing are quite similar to Pngcrush and figure 7.4. Once the tool has finished running, it will create an optimized file in the same directory as the tool.

7.4 Image Optimizer—a Visual Studio extension

Another great tool that's available as a Visual Studio plugin is Image Optimizer. Unlike the image optimization tools we've already covered in this chapter, it's an

```
Directory of C:\Users\Downloads\jpegtran

05/09/2012  19:56    <DIR>          .
05/09/2012  19:56    <DIR>          ..
16/08/2012  10:44            79,457 original.jpg
05/09/2012  19:55           151,552 jpegtran.exe
               2 File(s)        231,009 bytes
               2 Dir(s)  167,288,713,216 bytes free

C:\Users\Downloads\jpegtran>jpegtran -optimize original.jpg result.jpg
```

Figure 7.5 The command line settings for Jpegtran

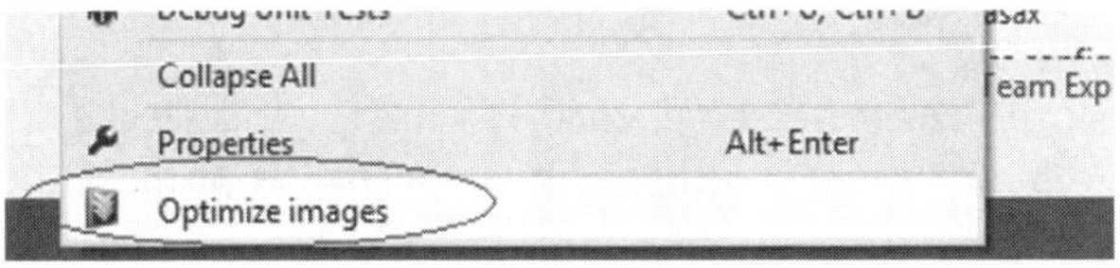

Figure 7.6   The right-click context menu that Image Optimizer generates. Simply select the image or folder and then choose Optimize images.

extension you can use from within the Visual Studio development environment. The extension adds a right-click context menu to any folder and image in your Solution Explorer and it allows you to automatically optimize all PNG, GIF, and JPEG files in that folder. The extension uses the Yahoo! Smush.it and PunyPNG tool to optimize the images. To download the extension, go to http://mng.bz/2MR6.

Figure 7.6 shows the right-click context menu that's available with the Image Optimizer extension. Once you download and install the extension, right-click a folder or individual image and select Optimize. The image(s) will be optimized automatically and you won't even need to leave Visual Studio.

While this tool is handy and enables you to optimize your images at the click of a button, you might find automating the updates using a command line tool is more effective depending on your environment setup and how often you change your images.

7.5   *Using data URIs*

So far you've learned about many of the tools you need in order to optimize your images and reduce their overall size. This reduction can go a long way toward reducing the total weight of your web pages, but what if there was a way to show these images without even making an HTTP request for them? It doesn't sound possible, but there is a sneaky trick you can apply using data URIs.

Data URIs are a scheme modern browsers use to read image objects that are embedded in a web page. Embedding data means the browser doesn't need to make an extra HTTP request to retrieve the image. The data URI scheme provides a way to include data in-line in web pages, as if they were external resources. You can actually embed the image in the page without having to make a request to the server! Instead of adding a reference to your image as a path or URL, you embed the image directly into the document using a Base64-encoded string. The data URI scheme can be applied to images in CSS, link tags, and image tags. The browser automatically understands the string and decodes it there and then instead of retrieving it via an HTTP request.

Normally you would reference an image in your HTML like so:

```
<img alt="Windows 8 Logo" src="/images/windows_logo.png" />
```

If you used data URIs, it would look something like this:

```
<img alt="Windows 8 Logo" src="data:image/png;base64, /9jAAQSkZJRg==)" />
```

The difference is the image can be decoded from the same page, meaning one less HTTP request and a faster page load time. In the sample that's provided, the data string is quite short, but you'll notice a much longer string if you're using a larger image.

You can achieve the same effect by using data URIs in CSS. You normally reference an image like this:

```
.logo {
background: url("/content/images/logo.png")
}
```

But you can reference the image like this with data URIs:

```
.logo {
background: url(data:image/gif;base64,R0lGODlhEAAQATWGVQ887AG)
}
```

Data URIs are a great way to reduce the overall page weight and the number of HTTP requests your web page is making. If your website focuses on mobile device usage, the fewer HTTP requests your website needs to make, the better the performance.

The advantages of using data URIs are:

- Data URIs reduce the number of HTTP requests.
- HTTP requests will be handled a lot faster.

Unfortunately, data URIs aren't without their limitations. As a rule, you should only use the data URI scheme when your images aren't too large. A large image will create a very long string in your HTML, and your string size might become significantly larger than the original image size! Other disadvantages of using data URIs are:

- No support in old versions of Internet Explorer.
- Base64-encoded data URIs are 1/3 larger in size than their binary equivalent, but this extra overhead is reduced to 0–10% if the HTTP server compresses the response with Gzip.
- Certain browsers have size limitations. (Internet Explorer 8 limits data URIs to a maximum size of 32 KB.)

As with most new features, some older browsers don't offer support, but it isn't as bad as you think—Firefox, Chrome, Opera, Safari, and IE8+ all offer support for data URIs. Another factor to consider is that you need to update the data URI every time you make a change to an image. This could become a maintenance nightmare if your website is image-intensive. The best way to handle this is to automate the data URI creation process. This is where ASP.NET comes in. You're about to learn about a technique that will enable you to apply automatic encoding logic to your images so you don't have to re-encode each time you update your image!

NOTE If you decide to use data URIs on your website, you should still try to optimize your images using the image optimization tools mentioned earlier. Reducing the image file sizes will also mean that you'll produce smaller Base64-encoded strings.

You may be wondering whether it's worth going to all this effort to produce data URIs automatically. You need to choose the code that applies to your situation best. If you

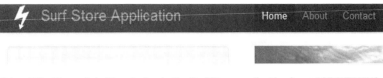

Figure 7.7   The updated header bar in the Surf Store application in an ASP.NET MVC application

find your images, icons, or logos don't change that often, you might be better off generating the data URI manually, but you won't get the benefit of browser detection logic. With a bit of clever caching, this code can produce lightning fast results and shave precious milliseconds from your page load time.

7.5.1 *Implementing data URIs in an ASP.NET MVC application*

HTML helpers in ASP.NET MVC can be a great way to quickly and easily apply repetitive server-side logic to operations on your Views. We're going to cover an example that will get you comfortable using the data URI scheme on your images in no time. The updates are going to be applied to the source code of the Surf Store application.

Figure 7.8   Adding a new class in the Solution Explorer

As the web developer for the Surf Store website, you've decided it needs a logo in the header bar. This is a great opportunity to use data URIs because the image is small and the technique will require one less HTTP request to the server. The HTML code in the Layout view has been updated to include a small logo, as shown in figure 7.7.

How do you make this update? Begin by navigating to your Solution Explorer and adding a class file called DataUriUtils.cs to the Utils folder (figure 7.8).

Inside the DataUriUtils.cs class file, add this code.

Listing 7.1   Checking to determine if the browser can handle data URIs

```
private static bool CanBrowserHandleDataUris()
{
    float browserVersion = -1;

    HttpRequest httpRequest = HttpContext.Current.Request;        Check to see if the
    HttpBrowserCapabilities browser = httpRequest.Browser;        browser is Internet
                                                                  Explorer
    if (browser.Browser == "IE")
    {
        browserVersion = (float) (browser.MajorVersion          Determine the
            + browser.MinorVersion);                            version of IE
    }
```

```
if (browserVersion > 8 || browserVersion == -1)
{
    return true;
}

return false;
}
```

◁── **If the IE version is higher than version 8, return true**

The code is used to determine if the user's browser is capable of handling data URIs. Earlier versions of IE aren't capable of handling data URIs. In order to serve the same experience to all users regardless of their browser, it's best if you check first. You want users with an older browser to see the images.

Next you need to perform a check to see if the file size is within a suitable boundary. Add the following code to the same class in your solution.

Listing 7.2 Determining if the browser can handle data URIs

```
private static bool IsFileSizeCorrect(string imageUrl)
{
string imagepath = HttpContext.Current.Server.MapPath(imageUrl);

// determine the length
long fileLength = new FileInfo(imagepath).Length;
return fileLength < 32768;
}
```

◁── **Determine the file length (size)**

◁── **If the file length is within the boundaries then return true, else return false.**

The code checks to see if the file size is less than 32 KB, and returns a Boolean value you'll use to decide whether to proceed with the optimization. If it returns true, then it will proceed and return a data URI image. If it is false, it will simply fall back and return the original image.

Now you need to convert the image to a Base64-encoded string. The code in the following listing uses the image URL and creates a Base64-encoded string based on the image that it reads.

Listing 7.3 Converting an image to a Base64-encoded string

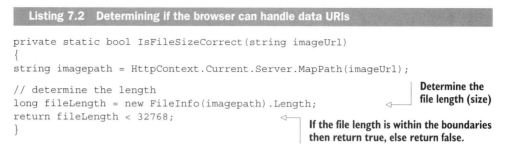

```
private static string ConvertImageToBase64String(string imageUrl)
{
    string imagepath = HttpContext.Current.Server.MapPath(imageUrl);
    using (Image image = Image.FromFile(imagepath))
    {
        using (MemoryStream memoryStream = new MemoryStream())
        {
            // Convert Image to byte[]
            image.Save(memoryStream, image.RawFormat);
            byte[] imageBytes = memoryStream.ToArray();

            // Convert byte[] to Base64 String
            string base64String = Convert.ToBase64String(imageBytes);
            return base64String;
        }
    }
}
```

Map the image to the current file path on the server

◁── **Read the image from disk based on this file path**

◁── **Convert the image object to a Base64-string**

Combining all the methods will return a chunk of image HTML and will be embedded in the page using the HTML Helper. You can use HTML Helpers to reduce the amount of tedious typing you must perform to create a standard HTML page.

The code in listing 7.4 uses the methods you've worked on and combines them to create your image HTML using data URIs. First, you use the two methods that you wrote in listings 7.1 and 7.2. This code checks if the file size isn't too large and also that the browser is capable of handling data URIs. You need to do this in order to serve the best experience to all users regardless of the browser that they are using. If the image passes the first two checks, the code converts the image to a Base-64 encoded string and builds an image tag with the data URI scheme and the Base-64 encoded string. If for any reason the image didn't meet the criteria, it will be returned as a standard image tag.

Listing 7.4   Creating a snippet of HTML to return in the HTML Helper

```
public static MvcHtmlString DrawImage(this HtmlHelper helper, string
    imageUrl, string alt)
{
if (CanBrowserHandleDataUris() && IsFileSizeCorrect(imageUrl))     ⟵   Determine if
{                                                                      the browser is
    // Get the file type                                              capable of
    string fileType = Path.GetExtension(imageUrl);                   handling data
    if (fileType != null)                                             URIs and if the
    {                                                                  file size isn't
        fileType = fileType.Replace(".", "");                         too large
    }
    // Convert the image                                          Convert the
    imageUrl = ConvertImageToBase64String(imageUrl);      ⟵       image to a Base64-
                                                                 encoded string
    return new MvcHtmlString(String.Format("<img alt=\"{0}\" " +
                        "src=\"data:image/{1};base64,{2}\" />",alt,
                        fileType, imageUrl));
}
                                                         If the image did
                                                         not meet the
return new MvcHtmlString(String.Format("<img alt=\"{0}\"    requirements, simply
⟹  src=\"{1}\" />", alt, imageUrl));              ⟵       return a standard
}                                                        HTML image tag.
```

Return a snippet of HTML that contains the Base64-encoded string ⟶

You now need to implement the code on your views. You're adding this change on the Layout view because it's being used for the standard layout for the logo across all views. Instead of creating a standard HTML image tag, you're going to use the HTML Helper that you created. The code in the next listing will create an HTML image tag if the image and the browser meet the requirements.

Listing 7.5   Implementing the HTML helper on the view

```
<div class="span3">
    <!-- Logo -->
<a href="/" class="logo_bar">
@Html.DrawImage(Url.Content(
```

```
➥  "~/content/images/store-logo.png"),
                "Surf Store Logo")
Surf Store Application</a>
</div>
```

⊲ ─── The HTML Helper will use the
image path and create a data URI
in the HTML image tag.

If you fire up the application and review the results of the HTML, it will look something like this:

```
<div class="span3">
<!-- Logo -->
<a href="/" class="logo_bar">
    <img alt="Surf Store Logo"
    src="data:image/png;base64,iVBORw0KGgo
    ➥ AAAANSUhEUgAAACg
    ➥ AAAAoCAYAAACM/A9
    ➥ Zoyj8pW/wfGAx77w
    ➥ dBG5WoOXAAAAAASU
    ➥ VORK5CYII=" />
    Surf Store Application</a>
</div>
```

By using this HTML helper to produce a data URI in the HTML, you've effectively created one less request for the browser.

If you compare the logo in the Surf Store application before and after applying the data URIs, you'll notice there is no visual difference whatsoever. The browser has interpreted the Base64-encoded string and converted it to the logo in figure 7.9.

7.5.2 Implementing data URIs in an ASP.NET Web Forms application

Using the power of the ASP.NET framework, data URIs can be easily implemented into a Web Forms application. The first thing you need to do is check to see if the user's browser is compatible with data URIs. Using ASP.NET, you can easily check the browser's capabilities and apply this logic on the server side, but it would be best if you had a method that simply produced the HTML you need and did the check at the same time.

In this example, you're going to make changes to the Surf Store application's source code. As the web developer on the site, you've decided it needs a logo in the header bar. This is a great opportunity to use data URIs because the image is small and this technique will require one less HTTP request to the server. The HTML code in the Master page has been updated to include a small logo, as shown in figure 7.10.

Next, navigate to your Solution Explorer and add a class file called DataUriUtils to the Utils folder (figure 7.11).

Inside the DataUriUtils.cs class file add the code in listing 7.6.

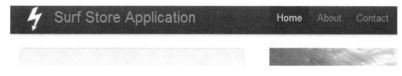

Figure 7.9 The result of the data URI image tag in the header

Surf Store Application
Home
About
Contact

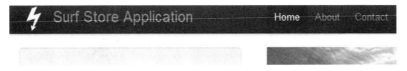

Figure 7.10 The updated header bar in the Surf Store application in an ASP.NET Web Forms application

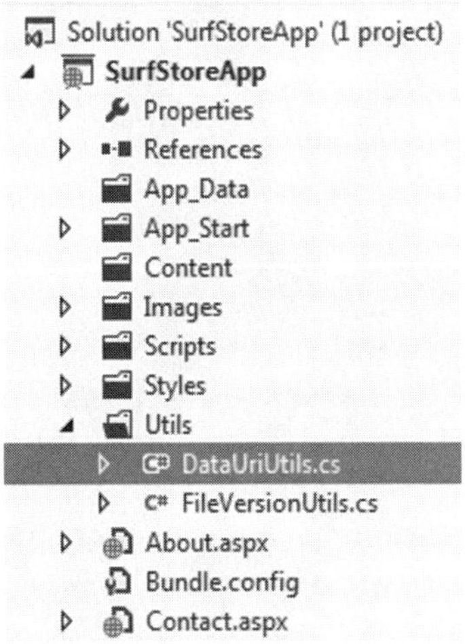

Solution 'SurfStoreApp' (1 project)
SurfStoreApp
Properties
References
App_Data
App_Start
Content
Images
Scripts
Styles
Utils
DataUriUtils.cs
FileVersionUtils.cs
About.aspx
Bundle.config
Contact.aspx

Figure 7.11 Add a new class file called DataUriUtils in the Solution Explorer

Listing 7.6 Checking to determine if the browser can handle data URIs

```
private static bool CanBrowserHandleDataUris()
{
    float browserVersion = -1;

    HttpRequest httpRequest = HttpContext.Current.Request;
    HttpBrowserCapabilities browser = httpRequest.Browser;

    if (browser.Browser == "IE")
    {
        browserVersion = (float)
        ➥ (browser.MajorVersion + browser.MinorVersion);
    }

    if (browserVersion > 8 || browserVersion == -1)
    {
        return true;
    }

    return false;
}
```

Check if the browser is IE.

Determine the version of IE.

If the IE version is greater than version 8, return true.

The code determines if the user's browser is capable of handling data URIs. Internet Explorer 8+ is capable of handling data URIs. You still want to serve the same experience to all users regardless of their browser, so it's best if you check first. You don't want some users on an older browser not to see the images! If the code detects an older browser, you return a standard image instead.

Next you need to check to see if the file size is within a suitable boundary. Add the following code to the same class in your solution.

Listing 7.7   Determining if the browser is capable of handling data URIs

```
private static bool IsFileSizeCorrect(string imageUrl)
{
string imagepath = HttpContext.Current.Server.MapPath(imageUrl);

// determine the length
long fileLength = new FileInfo(imagepath).Length;
return fileLength < 32768;
}
```

Determine the file length (size)

If the file length is within the boundaries then return true, else return false.

The code checks to see if the file size is less than 32 KB, and returns a Boolean value that you'll use to decide whether to proceed with the optimization.

Next, you need to convert the image to a Base64-encoded string. The code in the following listing uses the image URL and creates a Base64-encoded string based on the image that it reads.

Listing 7.8   Converting an image to a Base64-encoded string

```
private static string ConvertImageToBase64String(string imageUrl)
{
    string imagepath = HttpContext.Current.Server.MapPath(imageUrl);

    using (Image image = Image.FromFile(imagepath))
    {
        using (MemoryStream memoryStream = new MemoryStream())
        {
            // Convert Image to byte[]
            image.Save(memoryStream, image.RawFormat);
            byte[] imageBytes = memoryStream.ToArray();

            // Convert byte[] to Base64 String
            string base64String = Convert.ToBase64String(imageBytes);
            return base64String;
        }
    }
}
```

Map the image to the current file path on the server

Read the image from disk based on this file path

Convert the image object to a Base64 string

Finally, you wrap it all up. You can use all of the previous methods together to return a chunk of image HTML.

Listing 7.9   Creating a snippet of HTML to return as an HTML string

```
public static string DrawImage(string imageUrl, string alt)
{
    if (CanBrowserHandleDataUris() & IsFileSizeCorrect(imageUrl))
    {
        // Get the file type
```

Determine if the browser is capable of handling data URIs and if the file size isn't too large

```
        string fileType = Path.GetExtension(imageUrl);
        if (fileType != null)
        {
            fileType = fileType.Replace(".", "");
        }

        // Convert the image
        imageUrl = ConvertImageToBase64String(imageUrl);

        return String.Format("<img alt=\"{0}\" " +
"src=\"data:image/{1};base64,{2}\" />",
alt, fileType, imageUrl);
    }
return String.Format("<img alt=\"{0}\" src=\"{1}\" />", alt, imageUrl);
}
```

Return a snippet of HTML that contains the Base64-encoded string

Convert the image to a Base64-encoded string

If the image did not meet the requirements, simply return a standard HTML image tag.

The code in the listing uses the methods that you've worked on and combines them all to create your image HTML using data URIs. In order to serve the best experience to all browsers, the code checks if the file size isn't too large and if the browser is capable of handling data URIs. If the image passes the first two checks, the code then converts the image to a Base64-encoded string and builds an image tag using the data URI scheme and the Base64-encoded string. If for any reason the image did not meet the criteria, it will get returned as a standard image tag.

Now you need to implement this code in your web pages. I am adding this change on the Master page because it's being used as a standard layout for the logo across all pages. Instead of creating a standard HTML image tag, I am going to use static method that you created.

Listing 7.10   Implementing the static method on the web page

```
<div class="span3">
    <!-- Logo -->
<a href="/" class="logo_bar">
<%= DataUriUtils.DrawImage("Images/store-logo.png","Store Logo") %>
Surf Store Application</a>
</div>
```

The static method will use the image path and create a data URI in the HTML image tag.

The code in listing 7.10 will create an HTML image tag if the image and the browser meet the requirements. If you fire up the application and review the results of the HTML, it will look something like this HTML:

```
<div class="span3">
<!-- Logo -->
<a href="/" class="logo_bar">
    <img alt="Surf Store Logo"
    src="data:image/png;base64,iVBORw0KGgo
➥ AAAANSUhEUgAAACg
➥ AAAAoCAYAAACM/A9
➥ Zoyj8pW/wfGAx77w
➥ dBG5WoOXAAAAAASU
➥ VORK5CYII=" />
    Surf Store Application</a>
</div>
```

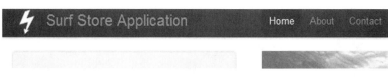

Figure 7.12   The result of the data URI image tag in the header in an ASP.NET MVC application

By using this HTML helper to produce a data URI within the HTML, you've effectively created one less request for the browser. Because the image is small enough, it hasn't had an impact on the overall size of the HTML.

When you compare the logo in the Surf Store application before and after applying the data URIs, you'll notice there is no visual difference. The browser has interpreted the Base64-encoded string and has converted it to the logo in figure 7.12.

7.6   *The importance of specifying image dimensions*

After you've processed and optimized the images in your web pages, look out for image dimensions in your HTML. It's easy to forget to specify the height and width of an image on your web page.

```
<img src="/Content/Images/image.jpg" />
```

The preceding code snippet is an example of an HTML image tag without the dimensions specified. It's important to specify the dimensions of an image because if a browser knows the dimensions of an element in a web page, it can begin rendering even before the images are downloaded. As the page is parsed and the browser begins laying it out, it needs to be able to flow around elements such as images. You'll even notice this appears as a suggestion when you profile your site using Google PageSpeed. Figure 7.13 shows the Google PageSpeed suggestion to specify image dimensions.

☑ Low priority (12)

   ⬭ Specify image dimensi...
   Defer parsing of JavaScript
   In-line Small CSS
   Serve scaled images
   Specify a cache validator
   Minify CSS
   Minify JavaScript
   Optimise images
   Minify HTML
   Remove query strings fro...
   Specify a Vary: Accept-...

Specify image dimensions

Specifying a width and height for all images allows for fast
Learn more

Suggestions for this page

The following image(s) are missing width and/or height att

- http://a43d55f6a02c4be185ce-9cfa4cf7c673a59966ac
- http://a43d55f6a02c4be185ce-9cfa4cf7c673a59966ac
- http://a43d55f6a02c4be185ce-9cfa4cf7c673a59966ac
- http://a43d55f6a02c4be185ce-9cfa4cf7c673a59966ac
- http://a43d55f6a02c4be185ce-9cfa4cf7c673a59966ac
- http://a43d55f6a02c4be185ce-9cfa4cf7c673a59966ac

Figure 7.13   Google PageSpeed suggests specifying the dimensions of an image to speed up page load times.

If dimensions aren't specified on the image tag, the browser will need to reflow and repaint once the image is downloaded. It's best if you specify your images similar to this code snippet:

```
<img src="/Content/Images/image.jpg" width="120" height="120" />
```

This simple change will allow the browser to render your page faster and begin displaying images and content to your users even before all the images are downloaded.

7.7   *The results*

Using the Surf Store application you've worked with throughout this book, you optimized and reduced the file size of the images using free tools that are available to download online. Next, you added a small logo to the Surf Store application and using data URIs you reduced any extra HTTP requests that needed to be made.

Now that you've made your improvements to the Surf Store application, you can compare the applications before and after performance. In this previous chapter, you looked into the advantages of using HTML5 in a web application. These advantages reduced the size of the HTML and after running the Surf Store application through the Google PageSpeed tool, the score on the home landing page came in at 91. Using the Yahoo! YSlow tool, the empty cache for the landing page showed 11 HTTP requests and a total page weight of 835 KB.

In this chapter, the total weight of the images on the landing page came to around 686 KB and 6 images in total. If you compare the changes after the image updates you've made in this chapter, the results are impressive (figure 7.14).

Wow! The overall PageSpeed score has jumped from 91 to 99 (out of 100). You've managed to make some pretty significant improvements to the overall load time and page speed. If you take a look at the Yahoo! YSlow results after making these changes, the results reveal similar gains (figure 7.15).

The Yahoo! YSlow performance score has also jumped up to 94, which is a significant improvement from 91. This is a solid result and you've significantly improved the performance score since you started out in chapter 3.

The chart in figure 7.16 shows that the overall image weight has also been reduced.

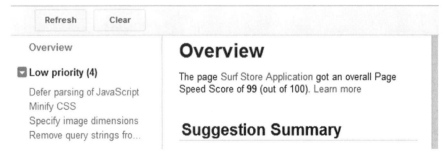

Figure 7.14   The PageSpeed score after applying the updates in this chapter

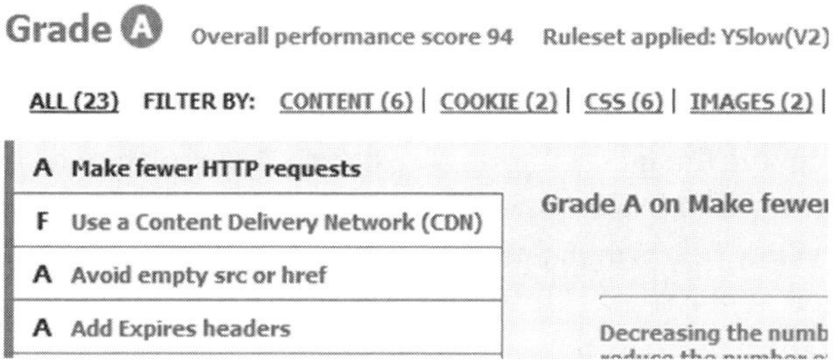

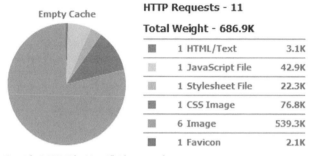

Figure 7.15 The Yahoo! YSlow score after making the image updates described in this chapter

Figure 7.16 The Yahoo! YSlow score after making the image updates described in this chapter

By applying the image optimization techniques you learned in this chapter, you've managed to cut about 147 KB from the image weight and therefore the total weight of the page. This is a significant reduction. If you applied these techniques to any site you're currently working on, you could produce even larger savings.

7.8 Summary

Images are often the heaviest components by weight in most web pages. By optimizing the images in your web pages, you can significantly reduce their size and reduce total page weight. In this chapter, you learned about freely available tools you can use to optimize your images and reduce their file size.

The image optimization tools you learned about in this chapter use lossless optimization, which won't affect the look or visual appearance of the images in any way. You learned about two online tools: Smush.it by Yahoo! and Kraken.io which allow you to optimize your images online and in batches. Another alternative is the ability to automate image optimization. Two tools you looked at were Jpegtran and Pngcrush—both are command line-based and are very effective at optimizing images. The final tool you learned about was the Image Optimizer for Visual Studio. It allows you to automate image optimization inside of Visual Studio with the click of a button.

Data URIs can be manually added to a web page, but in this chapter you learned a technique that allowed you to convert the image to a Base64-encoded string and embed the resource in the page automatically. The technique handles images that are updated frequently and makes sure you don't need to update your HTML each time the change takes place. The code takes support for older browsers into account, as well as images that might be too large.

This chapter was an important step in the overall performance improvement of your website. Optimizing the images in your website can save valuable bytes and improve your page load times radically. Even though you've produced great Google PageSpeed and Yahoo! YSlow performance scores thus far, you can take your website even further and produce better results! In the next chapter, you'll learn more about ETags and why they're important to web page performance.

ETags

This chapter covers

- ETags: what they are and why you should change them
- How browsers validate cache components
- Removing ETags in ASP.NET Web Forms and ASP.NET applications

In chapter 4, we examined and implemented HTTP Expires headers in an ASP.NET application. These HTTP headers tell the browser it can store certain components in its cache for a set amount of time, thereby reducing page load times because the browser doesn't need to retrieve these components from the server. In order to ensure the components are still valid, the browser makes a small validation request. In this chapter, you're going to investigate the ways the browser validates its cache components and what you can do to eliminate unnecessary HTTP requests.

ETags, also known as Entity Tags, are a protocol used for HTTP caching. They're unique strings that are sent back in the HTTP response that help the browser identify and validate the browser cache. If used incorrectly they can be inefficient, so in this chapter you're going to learn how to tweak your application so it performs at its best.

▼ Response Headers   view source
```
Cache-Control: public, max-age=88025
Connection: keep-alive
Content-Type: image/png
Date: Wed, 05 Dec 2012 05:30:53 GMT
ETag: 667f7454adb987cc384a59f5f3411ad7
Expires: Thu, 06 Dec 2012 05:57:58 GMT
Last-Modified: Thu, 29 Nov 2012 11:36:05 GMT
```

The ETag generated
by the server

Figure 8.1   The ETag is sent back by the server in an HTTP response.

8.1   What are ETags?

Every time you make an HTTP request for a resource on a web server, an ETag is
attached in the HTTP response data. These unique strings are used to identify the
cache and validate whether the cache in the user's browser matches the one on the
server. The browser cache can be much more efficient, and it saves bandwidth,
because the web server doesn't need to send a full response if the content hasn't
changed. In chapter 4, in the discussion of HTTP caching and the Expires header, you
learned that when you tell a browser to cache a resource in a web page, it stores it
along with an expiration date. The browser uses both the ETag and the Expires date
when validating the freshness of a resource.

Figure 8.1 shows an ETag in the Response header of a resource. The ETag shows
a simple string that looks similar to a GUID, a unique reference number often used
in software development. This unique string provides another way to validate
cached entries other than the last-modified date. It's stored against the resource in
the browser, and anytime you make an HTTP request for the same resource, it will
be sent in the HTTP headers of the request. ETags are similar to fingerprints
because they can be quickly compared to determine if two versions of a resource
are the same.

If you revisit a web page or refresh the page, the browser validates the resource
before reusing it by making a small HTTP request and sending up the ETag it's stored
against that resource, as illustrated in figure 8.2.

Figure 8.2 is a typical HTTP request header that contains an ETag. It's sent up in
the If-None-Match field and if the component hasn't expired in cache and it
matches what's on the server, the server returns an HTTP status code of 304 Not
Modified. This small check must be performed each time but it's much more

▼ Request Headers   view source
```
Accept: text/html,application/xhtml+xml,applicat
Accept-Charset: ISO-8859-1,utf-8;q=0.7,*;q=0.3
Accept-Encoding: gzip,deflate,sdch
Accept-Language: en-GB,en-US;q=0.8,en;q=0.6
If-Modified-Since: Thu, 29 Nov 2012 11:36:05 GMT
If-None-Match: 667f7454adb987cc384a59f5f3411ad7
```

The ETag

**Figure 8.2   An HTTP Request header containing the ETag that's stored against that
component. It's sent up in the If-None-Match field.**

Name Path	Method	Status Text	Type
:882/	GET	304 Not Modified	text/html
Css /Styles	GET	304 Not Modified	text/css
data:image/png;base...	GET	Success	image/png
surfing-homepage.png /Content/Images	GET	304 Not Modified	image/png
skate-homepage.png /Content/Images	GET	304 Not Modified	image/png
image.jpg /Content/Images	GET	304 Not Modified	image/jpeg

Figure 8.3 The network tab shows 304 HTTP statuses. The server returns this status code if the component is still valid and matches the ETag and last-modified date.

efficient than downloading the file with each HTTP request and receiving a 200 HTTP status code.

If you open your developer tools and analyze the network traffic, you might see something similar to figure 8.3. It shows a typical set of cached responses that return a 304 Not Modified HTTP code.

This unique string is sent back and forth between the server and browser, making ETags a flexible and efficient method of validating a cached component.

ETags aren't without their limitations. They rely on a hash algorithm to generate a unique string, and the outcome of this algorithm will differ depending upon which server you land. If you run your website across multiple servers with a load balancer (figure 8.4), you'll receive a different ETag on each server. The more servers you have

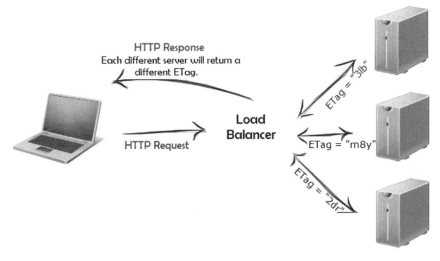

Figure 8.4 In a web farm environment, you'll get different ETags depending on which server you land on.

in a cluster, the lower the odds are that you'll share the same ETag across the servers. If each server uses a different ETag, the ETag won't validate against the component and it will need to perform a full HTTP request in order to update the component.

Figure 8.4 shows what happens when a user moves between servers in a multiweb server environment. The ETags returned by each server are different, even though the component is identical and should validate correctly. These extra requests are wasteful because you've done all the hard work and added HTTP Expires headers, but it won't validate if the ETag is different and a full HTTP request will have to be made.

What does this mean for you as a developer, and how can you make sure this doesn't happen? If you run your website in a web farm or load-balanced environment, it's best to remove the ETags altogether.

> **NOTE** If you're hosting your website on one server, it isn't necessary to remove ETags. The same ETag will be used every time and the validation check will take place efficiently and correctly. The rest of this chapter will have no bearing on your development and you should skip this step completely.

If you run your website through the Yahoo! YSlow performance tool, you may notice a recommendation similar to the one in figure 8.5.

This YSlow rule suggests you remove ETags if your websites are running in a web farm environment.

Figure 8.5   The Yahoo! YSlow rule recommends configuring ETags.

8.2   *Why should I change ETags?*

There has been a big debate surrounding ETags for a number of years. Some in the developer community say it's better to leave ETags in place because they're there for a reason. In 2006, Steve Souders wrote the original 14 rules for faster loading websites (table 2.2). It's not surprising that one of these original rules was the removal of ETags.

If you run your website in an environment with multiple servers, you'll come across the scenario where your users are served different ETags for the same component. It's even more prevalent today when many organizations run their websites in the cloud with multiple instances. Your users will notice slower page loads and your bandwidth will be wasted. You're looking to be as efficient as possible and avoid invalidating all of the work you've done on the HTTP Expires headers thus far.

If ETags are a method of validating a cache component and you remove it, how does the server know if the component is still valid? Even if the ETag is removed, the Last-Modified header will still validate the component based on its timestamp. By removing the ETag you're also effectively reducing the size of the header in the HTTP request and HTTP response. That's one less piece of data being passed back and forth from the server. In the remainder of this chapter, you're going to learn how to remove ETags in both ASP.NET Web Forms and ASP.NET MVC.

8.3   Removing ETags in ASP.NET Web Forms and ASP.NET MVC applications

Unfortunately there is no simple way to remove ETags in an ASP.NET application. Most of the IIS configuration work you've done thus far has been done inside an easy-to-use interface, but in order to make this change you'll need to create a custom module to remove the ETags. You'll practice this ETag removal technique on the Surf Store application you've been working on throughout this book.

The code for this chapter can be downloaded from the Github repository at https://github.com/deanhume/FastASPNetWebsites. Once you've downloaded the code, navigate to the chapter 8 folder and open the solution under your preferred development approach (Web Forms or MVC). The sample code you're about to run through can be applied to both ASP.NET Web Forms applications and ASP.NET MVC.

Figure 8.6   The custom module in the Surf Store application.

Start by adding a new class to the Utils folder, called ETagUtils.cs (figure 8.6).

Next, add the code in this listing to the class file.

Listing 8.1   A custom module to remove ETags

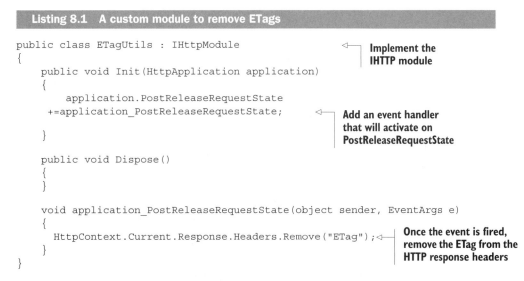

```
public class ETagUtils : IHttpModule                          ⊲⎤  Implement the
{                                                                 ⎦  IHTTP module
    public void Init(HttpApplication application)
    {
        application.PostReleaseRequestState
     +=application_PostReleaseRequestState;                   ⊲⎤  Add an event handler
                                                                 │  that will activate on
    }                                                            ⎦  PostReleaseRequestState

    public void Dispose()
    {
    }

    void application_PostReleaseRequestState(object sender, EventArgs e)
    {
        HttpContext.Current.Response.Headers.Remove("ETag");⊲⎤  Once the event is fired,
    }                                                          │  remove the ETag from the
}                                                              ⎦  HTTP response headers
```

First, the class is implementing the IHTTPModule interface. You need to do this in order to create a custom HTTP module. Next, an eventhandler is added for the PostReleaseRequestState. Once this event is fired, remove the ETag from the HTTP response header. The code will get fired across all requests and will occur every time a component is requested.

```
<!-- Etags -->
<modules>
  <add name="ETagUtils" type="SurfStoreApp.Utils.ETagUtils"/>
</modules>
</system.webServer>
```

Figure 8.7   Add the custom HTTP module that removes the ETags to the Web.config.

▼ **Response Headers**   view source

Accept-Ranges: bytes
Content-Length: 109038
Content-Type: image/png
Date: Sun, 16 Sep 2012 08:18:04 GMT
Expires: Tue, 22 Aug 2013 03:14:07 GMT
Last-Modified: Sun, 09 Sep 2012 07:56:40 GMT
Server: Microsoft-IIS/8.0
X-Powered-By: ASP.NET

Figure 8.8   The HTTP Response headers show that there are no more ETags.

As a last step, you need to add the custom module to the Web.config file. Figure 8.7 shows the configuration and where to place this file in your Web.config file.

If you fire up the application and observe the HTTP requests, you might notice something a little different.

Figure 8.8 shows the HTTP response headers for an image file the Surf Store application is requesting. There are no more ETags! You now send only one header instead of two and this prevents the cache from being invalidated.

8.4   *The results*

Using the code in this chapter, you configured and removed ETags from the Surf Store application. You did this with a custom HTTP module that removes the ETags from all HTTP header responses. In previous chapters, the Yahoo! YSlow tool issued a grade F for ETags, meaning the ETags weren't configured correctly and required some attention. The Yahoo! YSlow tool has a rule recommending ETag removal in an environment where a single web application is served across multiple servers. Before making these changes to the Surf Store application, the performance score on the Yahoo! YSlow tool came in at 94 out of 100 (figure 8.9).

If you run the sample application against the updated code in this chapter, the Yahoo! YSlow tool now reports an improved performance score (figure 8.10).

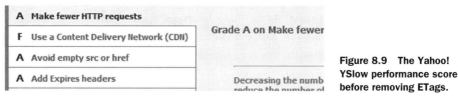

Figure 8.9   The Yahoo! YSlow performance score before removing ETags.

Grade Ⓐ Overall performance score 95   Ruleset applied: YSlow(V2)   URL: http://localhc

ALL (23)   **FILTER BY:**   <u>CONTENT (6)</u> | <u>COOKIE (2)</u> | <u>CSS (6)</u> | <u>IMAGES (2)</u> | <u>JAVASCRIPT (4)</u> | S

A Make fewer HTTP requests	
F Use a Content Delivery Network (CDN)	
A Configure entity tags (ETags)	**Grade A on Configure entity tags (ETags)**
A Add Expires headers	

Figure 8.10   **The Yahoo! YSlow performance score after removing ETags**

The result in figure 8.10 shows a grade A for configuring ETags, and the overall performance score has jumped to 95 out of 100. Although this only gave you a one-point increase in your performance score, it's a step in the right direction. Because you've made such major leaps in performance on the application thus far, further gains in performance are going to be a lot harder to obtain.

The performance cycle, discussed in chapters 1 and 6, plays an important role when you're optimizing a website. You should choose only the optimizations that are right for your situation and your development environment. In each chapter you've learned about the performance scores that both Yahoo! YSlow and Google PageSpeed offer. These tools are fantastic resources for analyzing your website's performance, but you should also allow them to help you improve your site's performance. Implementing performance improvements to your site requires analysis, so don't make changes only because these tools tell you to do so!

This is especially applicable to ETags. Although removing them altogether from your application may enhance its performance on a web farm, this may not be applicable to your server environment. The key here is to use the Identification step in the performance cycle. Use the technique that best suits your situation.

8.5   *Summary*

ETags offer a flexible and efficient way of validating components in a browser's cache. In certain circumstances, however, it's better to remove ETags if extra HTTP requests are required to validate the component. If your website is run in a web farm environment or if you load balance your website across multiple servers, each server might return a different ETag. In this chapter you learned how to remove ETags to prevent unnecessary HTTP requests from being made.

You learned how to remove ETags from both ASP.NET Web Forms and MVC applications with a custom HTTP module. This custom module was fired on each request and ensured that ETags were removed for each HTTP request that was made. By removing the ETags you improved the overall performance score of the Surf Store application and also ensured that your application made full use of the HTTP Expires headers.

Content Delivery Networks

This chapter covers

- CDN options
- Domain sharding
- Developing with a CDN

Every time you open a browser and request a URL, you're connecting to a server that could be located thousands of miles away. Each request you make might have to make a round-trip to a server that's halfway around the world! If you host your website in a data center in New York and a user connects to your site from Sydney, each HTTP request travels a very long distance. Each round-trip takes time, and even though it may only amount to milliseconds, it all adds up.

It's important to keep in mind who might be accessing your website—and from where. While the majority of users might be located in your own country, your website can be accessed by users who live elsewhere. A Content Delivery Network (CDN) allows users to access content on servers that are relatively close to them, minimizing the distance a request travels and reducing your site's web page load times. A CDN improves your chances of serving the same website experience to all your users, regardless of their location. Happy users = happy developers!

9.1   *What is a Content Delivery Network?*

Content Delivery Networks, or CDNs as they are better known, are a collection of server nodes located around the world that contain a clone of your site's static files. Because static files such as images, JavaScript, and CSS don't change often, they're ideal for CDNs.

Figure 9.1 shows a collection of nodes that might represent a typical CDN. Many CDN services will have a similar collection of nodes around the world. When you upload your content onto a CDN, it gets cloned and propagated to all the other servers in its network throughout the world. Each time a user requests one of these files, they get served the file from the node closest to them. If a user in Sydney requests a file, they will receive the file from a server in Sydney instead of a server in New York. This simple change is highly effective in reducing load times.

The benefits of using a CDN extend far beyond rapid response times. Using a CDN also reduces the number of requests served from your website, thereby reducing the amount of bandwidth your site requires. You'll still get all the benefits of caching and compression, along with a wider network that reduces the amount of bandwidth consumed by your website. But because your website's static content will be served from such a wide network, it also means your website's load will be well-balanced for your users, wherever they are around the world. Say, for example, you are about to launch a new product online and you expect a very high volume of traffic. This large, distributed network of nodes is much better equipped to handle high simultaneous traffic loads.

You might think only large companies can afford to use a CDN, but this is not the case. CDN technology is commercially available to all developers and it's affordable. You only pay for the file storage space and outgoing bandwidth that you use. I use an affordable and easy-to-use commercial CDN for my personal blog.

In chapter 2, you investigated WebPagetest, an online web performance tool that produces waterfall charts. WebPagetest is a great tool that allows you to run a free

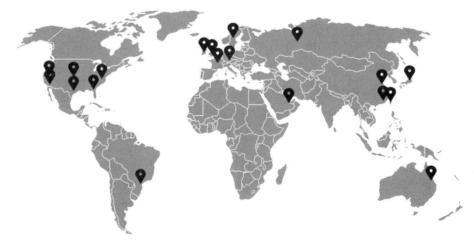

Figure 9.1   A typical collection of CDN nodes scattered in different locations around the world

website speed test from multiple locations around the globe. This is perfect if you need to test a CDN. I'll repeat: when you're developing your site, remember that users will be accessing your site from all over the world. It's important for you to give them the same speed and performance as the users who are close to the hosting server.

Let's take a look at how a CDN can improve your worldwide performance by using WebPagetest. First, navigate to www.webpagetest.org and enter the URL for my personal blog: www.deanhume.com. Choose a test location in Geneva, Switzerland, and choose IE8 as your test browser.

Once the test starts, it will be queued and run from that test location. When the test finishes running, you'll be presented with something similar to what you see in figure 9.2.

What you're looking for here is the location of the closest CDN node that served the static content. If you choose the first view (on an empty cache), and navigate to the request details, it will produce a table similar to figure 9.3.

In figure 9.3 notice the locations of the requests being served from the CDN. The test location is in Geneva, Switzerland, and the location of the files being served is Switzerland. Even though the dynamic content on my site is being hosted in a data-center in New York, I'm serving the static content to a Swiss user from a computer in Switzerland!

Now my Swiss user will receive their content from a server that is located geographically close to them, which saves a round-trip to a distant shore. Reducing the number of network hops also reduces latency, meaning you're able to speed up the time it takes for a web page to load.

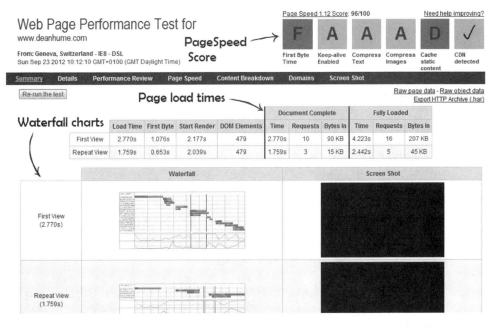

Figure 9.2 A web page performance test for www.deanhume.com against a test location in Geneva, Switzerland

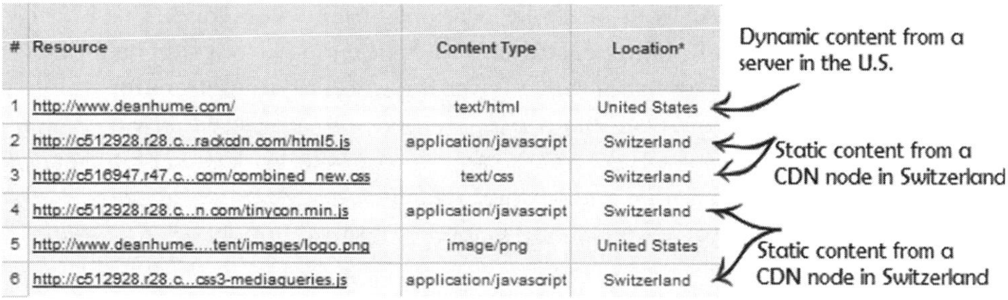

#	Resource	Content Type	Location*
1	http://www.deanhume.com/	text/html	United States
2	http://c512928.r28.c...rackcdn.com/html5.js	application/javascript	Switzerland
3	http://c516947.r47.c...com/combined_new.css	text/css	Switzerland
4	http://c512928.r28.c...n.com/tinycon.min.js	application/javascript	Switzerland
5	http://www.deanhume....tent/images/logo.png	image/png	United States
6	http://c512928.r28.c...css3-mediaqueries.js	application/javascript	Switzerland

Dynamic content from a server in the U.S.

Static content from a CDN node in Switzerland

Static content from a CDN node in Switzerland

Figure 9.3 The request details for deanhume.com against a test location in Geneva, Switzerland

9.2 CDN options

There are many CDN options available. Almost all of them are extremely easy to set up, and you can be up and running in minutes. Table 9.1 shows a few of my favorite commercial CDNs.

Table 9.1 A few more widely known commercial CDNs. Many companies offer an affordable CDN service.

CDN Name	Website
Amazon Cloudfront	http://aws.amazon.com/cloudfront/
Rackspace CDN	www.rackspace.com/cloud/public/files/
Windows Azure CDN	www.windowsazure.com
Akamai CDN	www.akamai.com/
CacheFly	www.cachefly.com/
EdgeCast	www.edgecast.com/
GoGrid CDN	www.gogrid.com/products/infrastructure-cdn

Each commercial CDN offers a competitive pricing structure as well as a dedicated network infrastructure. Because each company has its own requirements, specific CDN setup techniques will be left for you to discover.

You shouldn't feel constrained by my favorites in table 9.1. If you discover other CDN providers, investigate them, try them out. Go out and get a CDN! It will make a big difference to your website's performance around the world. CDN storage is cheap, so play with a few of them and choose the CDN that best suits your needs and budget.

9.3 Domain sharding

In chapter 6 you learned HTML optimization techniques to help you improve how a browser renders your web pages. One topic was the browser's ability to download a web page's components in parallel. Most browsers limit the number of parallel connections opened to a particular domain. Figure 9.4 shows a browser downloading two

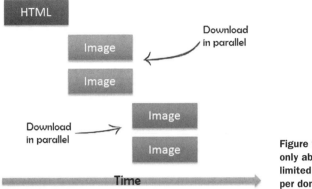

Figure 9.4 Most browsers are only able to download from a limited number of connections per domain.

images at a time in parallel. To overcome this limitation, you can apply a technique called domain sharding, which splits resources across domains. If a browser allows a limited number of connections per domain, add another domain with a CDN. The CDN is as another domain from which you're serving static content. Newer browsers allow a much higher number of parallel downloads, but this technique is still recommended because you get the added benefits of a CDN as well as a higher number of parallel downloads for older browsers.

Figure 9.5 contains a snapshot of the network components for Amazon.com. Note that in the figure the main HTML web page is being downloaded from www.amazon .com, yet the static files are being downloaded from two separate domains. From a simple investigation of the network downloads, it seems that the three following domains are being used to serve the static content from amazon.com:

- Amazon.com
- G-ecx.images-amazon.com
- Z-ecx.images-amazon.com

Name Path	Method	Status Text	Type
www.amazon.com	GET	200 OK	text/html
BeaconSprite-US-01._V394051227_.png g-ecx.images-amazon.com/images/G/01/gno/be	GET	200 OK	image/png
site-wide-7681525081._V1_.css z-ecx.images-amazon.com/images/G/01/brows	GET	200 OK	text/css
transparent-pixel._V192234675_.gif g-ecx.images-amazon.com/images/G/01/x-local	GET	200 OK	image/gif
BTS_towels_roto_300x75._V142687074_.gif g-ecx.images-amazon.com/images/G/01/img12/	GET	200 OK	image/gif

Figure 9.5 A snapshot of the network components that are downloaded when you visit www.amazon.com.

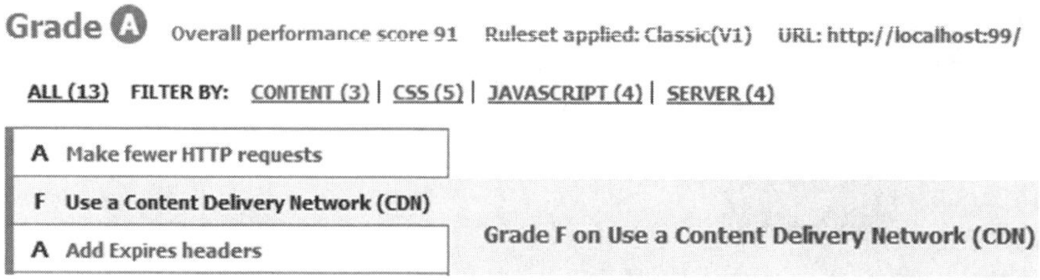

Grade Ⓐ Overall performance score 91   Ruleset applied: Classic(V1)   URL: http://localhost:99/

ALL (13) FILTER BY: CONTENT (3) | CSS (5) | JAVASCRIPT (4) | SERVER (4)

| A Make fewer HTTP requests |
| F **Use a Content Delivery Network (CDN)** |
| A Add Expires headers |

Grade F on Use a Content Delivery Network (CDN)

Figure 9.6   The Yahoo! YSlow score for the Surf Store application still needs some improvement.

Yahoo! released a study in 2007 that recommends sharding across at least two domains.[1] The study notes that performance starts to degrade above four domains; that's why a good compromise is two domains. Maximizing parallel downloads comes at a cost, and depending on your bandwidth and CPU speed, too many parallel downloads can degrade performance.

CDNs are becoming more and more affordable and freely available. You'll find many of the top-performing websites today use domain sharding to provide a faster platform for their static content. If you combine the power of a CDN's geographical node base with the browser's ability to download more efficiently from multiple domains, your website's load times will drastically improve. This improvement will be observed across all browsers, both old and new.

9.4   *Developing with a CDN*

If you open the Surf Store application and run it against the Yahoo! YSlow web performance tool, the performance score for the site is 91 out of 100. This is a good score, but the tool grades each suggestion separately, so you still score an F for a Content Delivery Network. I reckon we can do better! Figure 9.6 shows the result that the Yahoo! YSlow tool produces.

Adding your website components to a CDN is an easy transition. But depending on your development environment, it may not always be advisable to work directly off a CDN while your website is still under development. You may have a development team that needs to access these files constantly, which can add to your bandwidth bills. It's best to work off local copies while in development, then switch to the CDN once the website is in production. Next, you'll learn a technique in both ASP.NET MVC and ASP.NET Web Forms that will allow you to work with a CDN while still in development.

9.4.1   *ASP.NET MVC HTML helper for CDN development*

You can add an HTML helper to your sample application that contains a switch between your development content and the production content on a CDN. Whether or not you

---

[1] Tenni Theurer, "Performance Research, Part 4: Maximizing Parallel Downloads in the Carpool Lane," YUI blog, April 11, 2007, http://yuiblog.com/blog/2007/04/11/performance-research-part-4/.

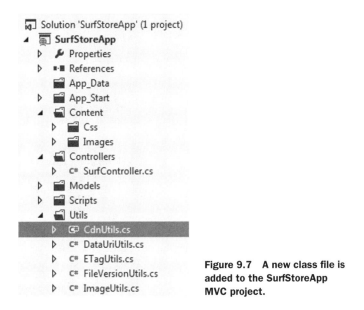

Figure 9.7 A new class file is added to the SurfStoreApp MVC project.

work on a team, it can still be beneficial to use development content before moving to production content when your site goes live. The key to using this technique is matching the local file structure to that of your CDN. This makes it easier to navigate between folders and allows you to easily map to certain files. Let's run through an example that makes use of this technique.

Begin by adding a key to the Web.config file with the location of the CDN.

Listing 9.1 Adding the CDN URL to the Web.config file

```
<appSettings>
    <add key="CDNUrl" value=" http://8860072f33207da70357-     ⟵  The URL
       90a4bb029bba92ae45972910051b9367                          of the CDN
       .r47.cf3.rackcdn.com "/>
</appSettings>
```

You added the CDN URL to the `appSettings` section of the Web.config file. Next you're going to use this CDN URL to build a path for your content, depending on whether you're in Release or Debug mode. Start by adding a new class file, called CdnUtils.cs, to the solution. Figure 9.7 shows the newly created class file in the Solution Explorer of the sample application.

Inside this new class, add the code in the following listing.

Listing 9.2 Using the CDN URL in Debug/Release mode

```
/// <summary>
/// This extension method is used to generate a URL path
/// for the CDN depending whether or not we are in release
/// or debug mode.
/// </summary>
```

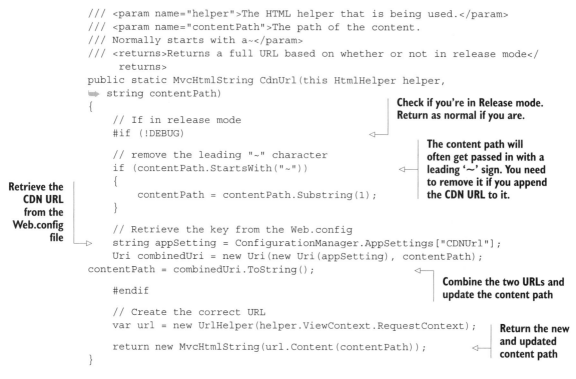

```
/// <param name="helper">The HTML helper that is being used.</param>
/// <param name="contentPath">The path of the content.
/// Normally starts with a~</param>
/// <returns>Returns a full URL based on whether or not in release mode</
      returns>
public static MvcHtmlString CdnUrl(this HtmlHelper helper,
    string contentPath)
{
    // If in release mode
    #if (!DEBUG)

    // remove the leading "~" character
    if (contentPath.StartsWith("~"))
    {
        contentPath = contentPath.Substring(1);
    }

    // Retrieve the key from the Web.config
    string appSetting = ConfigurationManager.AppSettings["CDNUrl"];
    Uri combinedUri = new Uri(new Uri(appSetting), contentPath);
contentPath = combinedUri.ToString();

    #endif

    // Create the correct URL
    var url = new UrlHelper(helper.ViewContext.RequestContext);

    return new MvcHtmlString(url.Content(contentPath));
}
```

Check if you're in Release mode. Return as normal if you are.

The content path will often get passed in with a leading '~' sign. You need to remove it if you append the CDN URL to it.

Retrieve the CDN URL from the Web.config file

Combine the two URLs and update the content path

Return the new and updated content path

The code uses the content path that is passed in and updates it with the CDN URL, depending on whether the code is in Release mode. If you're still in Debug mode, the code will run as normal and return the content path that was passed in. Only if you're in Release mode will the CDN URL be appended to the content path.

Finally, update your views to use the new HTML helper method you wrote. Instead of calling an HTML image tag like so:

```
<img src="@Url.Content("~/Content/Images/surfing-homepage.png")" />
```

You now use:

```
<img src="@Html.CdnUrl("~/Content/Images/surfing-homepage.png")" />
```

And that will produce the following HTML when the web page is rendered:

```
<img src="http://88600723r47.cf3.rackcdn.com/Content/Images/
surfing-homepage.png" />
```

This HTML helper will allow you to switch easily between the CDN and your local file storage.

9.4.2   *ASP.NET Web Forms helper for CDN development*

Whether or not you work in a team environment, it can still be beneficial to use local content before moving to using CDN content when your site goes live. The key to using this technique is matching the local file structure to that of your CDN. This

```
Solution 'SurfStoreApp' (1 project)
  SurfStoreApp
    Properties
    References
    App_Data
    App_Start
    Images
    Scripts
    Styles
    Utils
        CDNUtils.cs
      C#  DataUriUtils.cs
      C#  ETagUtils.cs
      C#  FileVersionUtils.cs
    About.aspx
    Contact.aspx
    Default.aspx
    Global.asax
    packages.config
    Product.aspx
    Site.Master
    Web.config
```

Figure 9.8   A new class file is added to the SurfStoreApp project.

makes it easier to navigate between folders and allows you to easily map to certain files. You're about to run through an example using ASP.NET that uses this technique.

Start by adding a key to the Web.config file with the location of the CDN.

Listing 9.3   Adding the CDN URL to the Web.config

```
<appSettings>
<add key="CDNUrl" value=" http://8860072f33207da70357-      ◁──  The URL of
    90a4bb029bba92ae45972910051b9367.r47.cf3.rackcdn.com "/>      the CDN
</appSettings>
```

You added the CDN URL to the Web.config file's `appSettings` section. Next you're going to use the CDN URL to build a path for your content depending on whether you're in Release or Debug mode. Start off by adding a new class file called CdnUtils.cs to the solution. Figure 9.8 shows the newly created class file in the Solution Explorer of the sample application.

Inside this new class, add this code.

Listing 9.4   Using the CDN URL in Debug/Release mode

```
/// <summary>
/// This extension method is used to generate a URL path
/// for the CDN depending whether or not we are in release
/// or debug mode.
/// </summary>
```

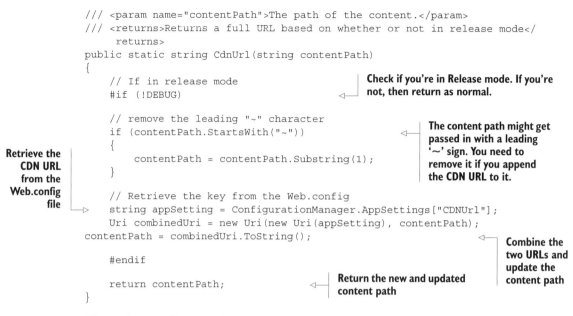

```
/// <param name="contentPath">The path of the content.</param>
/// <returns>Returns a full URL based on whether or not in release mode</
       returns>
public static string CdnUrl(string contentPath)
{
    // If in release mode
    #if (!DEBUG)

    // remove the leading "~" character
    if (contentPath.StartsWith("~"))
    {
        contentPath = contentPath.Substring(1);
    }

    // Retrieve the key from the Web.config
    string appSetting = ConfigurationManager.AppSettings["CDNUrl"];
    Uri combinedUri = new Uri(new Uri(appSetting), contentPath);
contentPath = combinedUri.ToString();

    #endif

    return contentPath;
}
```

Check if you're in Release mode. If you're not, then return as normal.

The content path might get passed in with a leading '~' sign. You need to remove it if you append the CDN URL to it.

Retrieve the CDN URL from the Web.config file

Combine the two URLs and update the content path

Return the new and updated content path

The code uses the passed in content path and updates it with the CDN URL, depending on whether or not the code is in Release mode. If you're still in Debug mode, the code will run as normal and return the content path that was passed in. The CDN URL will be appended to the content path only if you're in Release mode.

Finally, you need to update your views to use the new helper method that you wrote. Instead of calling an HTML image tag like so:

```
<img src="Images/surfing-homepage.png" />
```

You now use:

```
<img src="<%= SurfStoreApp.Utils.CdnUtils.CdnUrl("Images/
surfing-homepage.png") %>" />
```

This will produce the following HTML when the web page is rendered:

```
<img src="http://88600723r47.cf3.rackcdn.com/
➥ Content/Images/surfing-homepage.png" />
```

By making this simple change, you're making sure you're developing and using local content first; this might save you a hefty CDN bill!

9.5   *The results*

You have updated the Surf Store application in both solutions (MVC and Web Forms) to use the new CDN for its static content. When you ran the sample application against the Yahoo! YSlow tool, the previous performance score came in at 91 out of 100. Before running YSlow against the sample application again, you need to tell YSlow the name of your CDN. The tool doesn't have a known list of CDNs it uses to validate

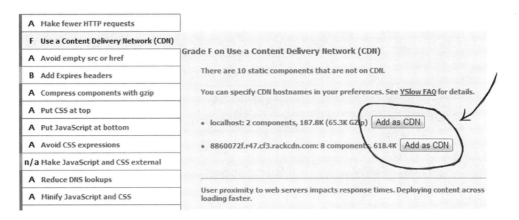

Figure 9.9 The latest YSlow performance result. The YSlow tool gives you the ability to add your own CDNs to a list of approved CDNs .

against, but it does give you the option to add your own CDNs to the list. In figure 9.9, the YSlow tool has detected that content is being served from two servers. In this case, you'll add the CDN but nothing else from the local host, as this would most likely be our hosting server.

Once the CDN has been added to the list and the tool is rerun, the performance score improves. Figure 9.10 shows you now have an overall performance score of 99 out of 100! The CDN rule suggestion has gone from an F to an A.

If you run the Surf Store website against the Google PageSpeed tool, you'll get a similar result. Figure 9.11 shows a performance score of 99 out of 100! This is pretty impressive considering we've taken this website from a starting score of 57 to a score of 99 out of 100.

Grade 🅐 Overall performance score 99   URL: http://localhost:999/

ALL (22) FILTER BY: CONTENT (6) | COOKIE (2) | CSS (6) | IMAGES (2) | JAVASCRIPT (4) | SERVER (5)

A Make fewer HTTP requests	
A Compress components with gzip	**Grade A on Make fewer HTTP requests**
A Avoid CSS expressions	
A Minify JavaScript and CSS	Decreasing the number of components on a page re
A Configure entity tags (ETags)	reduce the number of components include: combine
A Reduce the number of DOM elements	Sprites and image maps.
A Use cookie-free domains	»Read More
A Make favicon small and cacheable	

Figure 9.10 The YSlow performance score after moving the content onto a CDN

Figure 9.11 The Google PageSpeed score after moving the static content to a CDN.

9.6 *Summary*

Every time you open a web page, you could be making a round-trip to a server halfway around the world to retrieve the required components to load the page. These round-trips take time, and not surprisingly, the farther away you are from the hosting server, the longer it will take to download the web page components. You can improve this delay with a CDN.

In this chapter you've learned about the benefits of using a CDN to serve static components to your users from a server that is geographically closer to them. Instead of making a round-trip to a server that could be many miles away, your users will receive content from a server node that is a lot closer. You've learned about domain sharding and how you can use it to overcome the browser's limits when it comes to downloading multiple resources in parallel. By using an extra domain for your site, the browser is able to download more components in parallel. A CDN can also be a great way to add an extra domain to your application that will help with domain sharding. In this chapter we implemented a technique in the Surf Store application that allowed you to easily switch between the content on a CDN and the local content while your site is in development. This technique will hopefully save you money on your CDN bandwidth bills.

Our Surf Store application now has an overall performance score of 99 out of 100 across both the Google PageSpeed and Yahoo! YSlow tools. Not bad considering we started off with a lowly 57 out of 100. The overall load time of the page has been cut in half and the total page weight was also reduced significantly. In the next part of this book, we shift our focus toward server-side code and look at ways that we can leverage the power of the server to further improve page performance.

Part 3

ASP.NET–
specific techniques

Until now, the focus of this book has been on front-end performance and why the Performance Golden Rule plays a major part in improving page load times. In part 3, you'll look deeper into the internals of the ASP.NET framework and see how you can harness its features to improve the performance of your applications.

In these final chapters, you'll look at both ASP.NET MVC and ASP.NET Web Forms and understand the nuances that each framework might offer and how you can configure your application for optimal performance. As you begin to focus your attention on the back-end code, you may notice that identifying bottlenecks in your code isn't easy.

You will discover profiling tools to help you pinpoint exact lines of code that may be slowing down your application. You will learn how to integrate a free profiler into both ASP.NET MVC and ASP.NET Web Forms applications.

In chapter 12, you will cover data caching and how it can be implemented and used effectively. The .NET framework has built-in support for caching that you can use to cache frequently accessed data so as to limit the load on your servers.

You will review the Surf Shop application that has been used throughout this book and look at the performance of the application as a whole. You will be surprised to learn that you managed to halve the load time of certain pages using the techniques that we have built on in each chapter.

Tweaking ASP.NET MVC performance

This chapter covers

- Fine tuning ASP.NET MVC
- Using view engines
- Release mode versus Debug mode
- The importance of a favicon
- Utilizing a code profiler

According to the Performance Golden Rule, 80 to 90% of end-user response time is spent on the front end, and so far we've been focusing our efforts on optimizing front-end code. The Surf Store application had a very poor end-user response time originally, but you've optimized it over the course of this book until you cut its response time in half! But, what happens when your application continues to run slowly despite having a highly optimized front end? Sometimes you can't avoid the fact that something in the back-end code is affecting your application's performance.

In this chapter, you're going to shift your focus from front end-specific techniques to ASP.NET MVC-specific techniques. (Chapter 11 will focus on ASP.NET Web Forms performance.) We'll use a little fine-tuning to squeeze precious milliseconds out of your ASP.NET MVC application and we'll begin to scrutinize the framework more closely. When you create a new ASP.NET MVC project in Visual Studio, it's filled with loads of useful coding helpers that make your life as a developer easier. You're about to learn tips and tricks you can apply to your ASP.NET MVC application that will help it run more efficiently. Aside from improved page load times, you'll also reduce the memory footprint on your servers, which is exactly what you need if your site experiences a high level of traffic.

You'll also use a web page profiler to help you identify bottlenecks and areas for improvement. This profiling tool is different from the tools we've used so far because it will integrate with the back-end code and pinpoint the exact pieces of code that may be causing bottlenecks in your application. The tool is open source and easy to use. You'll be set up and profiling in about 5 minutes!

10.1   Using only the view engines that you need

By default, ASP.NET MVC ships with two view engines: the Web Forms view engine and the Razor view engine. When you create a new MVC project, you're given the choice of view engines (figure 10.1).

By default, both engines are included in the application startup. ASP.NET MVC resolves named views by searching first for files that match the Web Forms view engine's naming conventions. If your MVC application can't find a view, the error message in figure 10.2 might be a familiar sight.

Each time MVC looks for a view, it searches all those locations until it finds what it's looking for. In figure 10.2 you'll see that the Razor view is the fifth view to be searched for after ASP.NET MVC fails to find the first few views. Extra lookups take time, but if you remove all other view engines that are available at application startup, and are left with only the view engine that you need, MVC doesn't have to

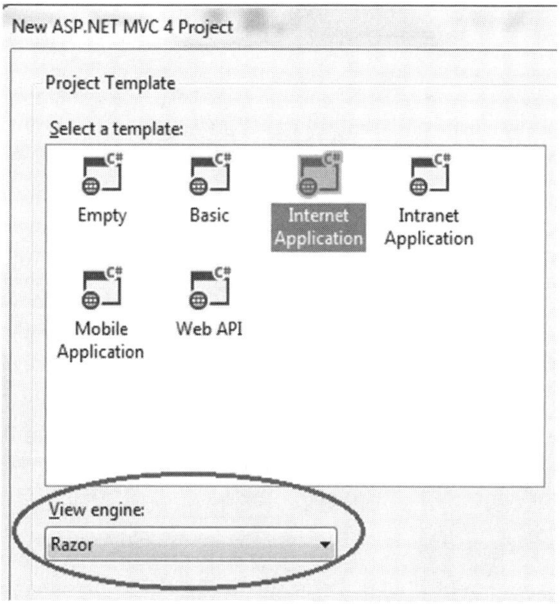

Figure 10.1   When you create a new ASP.NET MVC project, you have a choice of view engines.

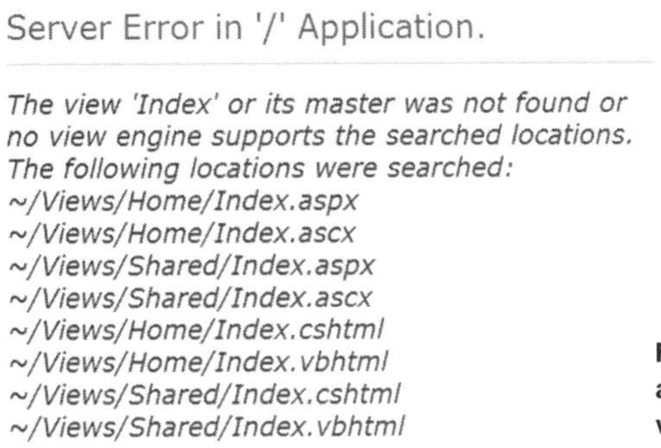

Server Error in '/' Application.

The view 'Index' or its master was not found or
no view engine supports the searched locations.
The following locations were searched:
~/Views/Home/Index.aspx
~/Views/Home/Index.ascx
~/Views/Shared/Index.aspx
~/Views/Shared/Index.ascx
~/Views/Home/Index.cshtml
~/Views/Home/Index.vbhtml
~/Views/Shared/Index.cshtml
~/Views/Shared/Index.vbhtml

**Figure 10.2   By default, an ASP.NET MVC
application must search across multiple
view engine locations to find a view.**

waste time searching all the other locations. If you intend to use only one type of view
engine throughout your code, make sure there's only one view engine available for
the application to search. Fortunately, ASP.NET MVC is configurable and lets you update
your view engines.

In your application, begin by opening up the Global.asax file.

Listing 10.1   Remove unused view engines in your Global.asax file

```
protected void Application_Start()
{
 ViewEngines.Engines.Clear();
 ViewEngines.Engines.Add(new
   RazorViewEngine());

    AreaRegistration.RegisterAllAreas();

    WebApiConfig.Register(GlobalConfiguration.Configuration);
    FilterConfig.RegisterGlobalFilters(GlobalFilters.Filters);
    RouteConfig.RegisterRoutes(RouteTable.Routes);

    BundleConfig.RegisterBundles(BundleTable.Bundles);
}
```

**Add this code to the Global.asax file to
remove all other view engines. You start
by clearing all view engines.**

**Add the view engine you want to
use. In this case it's Razor.**

The code starts by clearing out all the available default engines. Next, add the view
engine you're using in the application. In this case it's Razor, but it could easily be the
Web Forms view engine or a custom view engine.

By making this small change to your application, you've reduced the number of
locations the MVC routing system needs to check before it finds a match and you've
reduced the time it takes for a view to be returned to the user.

10.2   *Release mode vs. Debug mode*

If you're about to deploy your website to a production environment, one of the most
important things you can do is to make sure it's been compiled and deployed in
Release mode. You may be familiar with the compilation configuration drop-down
in Visual Studio, shown in figure 10.3.

As the name states, Debug mode is meant for debugging and is meant to make
your life as a developer a lot easier. Visual Studio's built-in debugger allows you to

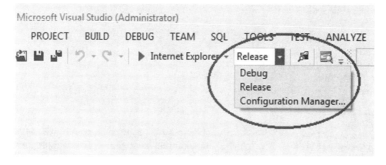

Figure 10.3   Visual Studio allows you to publish your code in two different modes: Debug and Release.

pause and step through code so you can debug and visualize the values in your application. Unfortunately, Debug mode isn't ideal for code performance. When your code is running in Debug mode, a number of nonoptimal things are happening:

- Code executes more slowly because additional debug paths are enabled.
- More memory is used within the application at runtime.
- ASP.NET MVC takes longer to resolve a view name.
- Certain timeouts are disabled, so you're blind to any long-running operations that should have timed out.
- The bundling and minification code you wrote in chapter 5 won't be enabled because it must run in Release mode.

In Debug mode, ASP.NET MVC has optimized the view resolution to simplify development. MVC iterates through the views and attempts to resolve them every time your code renders a view. This makes your life as a developer a lot easier because the development environment responds immediately to any changes you've made. But in Release mode, everything is optimized for performance. MVC resolves a view more efficiently because it caches the result of the lookup. A new view is cached automatically when it's resolved in Release mode, dramatically speeding up the response time since the code doesn't need to perform another disk read.

If you'd like to know whether your application is running in Debug mode, check the Web.config file. You might notice something similar to the next listing.

Listing 10.2   A Web.config file with `debug=true` **attribute**

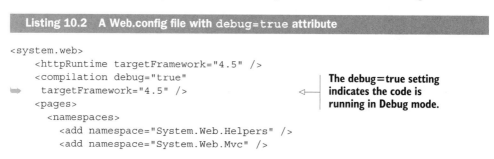

```
<system.web>
    <httpRuntime targetFramework="4.5" />
    <compilation debug="true"
    targetFramework="4.5" />
    <pages>
      <namespaces>
        <add namespace="System.Web.Helpers" />
        <add namespace="System.Web.Mvc" />
```

The debug=true setting indicates the code is running in Debug mode.

```
        <add namespace="System.Web.Mvc.Ajax" />
        <add namespace="System.Web.Mvc.Html" />
        <add namespace="System.Web.Routing" />
        <add namespace="System.Web.WebPages" />
    </namespaces>
  </pages>
</system.web>
```

It isn't ideal to run your application in Debug mode in a production environment. The preferred way to switch to Release mode is to deploy your application with Visual Studio and publish it in Release mode. You could also remove `debug=true` from your Web.config file so the application pool in IIS will recycle and the application will then run in Release mode.

This setting is highly important. If you're running your application in Debug mode in a production environment, it's almost definitely running slower than necessary, so make sure you publish your application in Release mode.

10.3 The importance of a favicon

You may be familiar with the 16 x 16 image that appears on the address bar when you browse a website. This tiny image, known as a *favicon*, is often used to display the logo of an organization or an image you would associate with the brand you're viewing. Figure 10.4 shows an example of two favicons in the Google Chrome browser.

By default, most modern browsers look for a favicon, so turning it off isn't an option. The browsers look in the root of the application for the path `/favicon.ico` and if they don't find it, they return a 404 error. Fortunately, these 404 errors occur silently on your server and aren't shown to your users. You might only pick up the error with the correct error logging tools on the server. How does this affect your application? The 404 error page is larger than a favicon, so the client spends time downloading an error page which is larger and takes more time to download than the favicon itself. Forgetting to add a favicon might cause extra disk I/O and computation, all of which adversely affect response times and increase server load.

One of my most memorable stories about favicons is the story behind the success of Instagram. During the early stages of Instagram, the website started to receive up to 25,000 sign-ups a day! The back-end engineers noticed that the error logs on the server had a lot of 404 errors coming from a missing favicon. These 404 errors were causing unnecessary disk reads that were negatively impacting the server's load. As soon as the favicon was added, the 404 errors stopped and a huge burden was instantly lifted off the server. Instagram has over 100 million registered users today. Imagine the impact a missing favicon would have on their servers now.

| W Favicon - Wikipedia, the fr ✕ | ● Surf Store Application ✕ |

Figure 10.4 The active tab shows the favicon for the Surf Store application. The inactive tab shows the favicon for the Wikipedia website.

It's best to include a favicon in the root of your MVC application, but if you choose to include the favicon in another location, you may notice an interesting error in your error logs.

The controller for path /favicon.ico does not implement IController.

Fortunately, this error will occur in the background and won't be shown to the user. Because of the nature of MVC, instead of looking for a normal icon file in the root of your application, the ASP.NET MVC routing will be used. The favicon.ico is regarded as a path and the MVC routing will look for a controller called favicon.ico first. Now your application is taking a double performance hit. Instead of performing a simple I/O operation, the icon request is hitting code and making the application work harder than it needs to.

If you still choose not to include a favicon in the root of your application, the following listing contains code that tells ASP.NET MVC to ignore the route.

Listing 10.3   Ignoring the favicon in the RouteConfig.cs file

```
public class RouteConfig
{
    public static void RegisterRoutes(RouteCollection routes)
    {
        routes.IgnoreRoute("{resource}.axd/{*pathInfo}");

            routes.MapRoute(
            name: "Default",
            url: "{controller}/{action}/{id}",
            defaults: new { controller = "Surf",
                            action = "Index",
                            id = UrlParameter.Optional }
        );

        // Ignore the favicon
        routes.IgnoreRoute("favicon.ico");          ◁⎯⎯  Add this line of code to
                                                         ignore the favicon.
    }
}
```

The code will ignore the route and save that extra bit of work being done on the server. Although you've made sure you aren't producing tons of 404 errors on the server, and extra work isn't being performed by the server in vain, this line of code doesn't necessarily make your website faster. The code makes sure the server won't waste its resources executing code and looking for a file unnecessarily, helping you keep your application efficient and running smoothly, but you may still want to consider adding a favicon to your application. This won't give you an instant performance benefit, but instead a long-term performance gain that will ensure that high traffic won't affect the overall performance of your application.

Unfortunately, these favicon problems extend to other types of icons. A wide range of mobile devices that browse your website will look for a new type of icon called a web clip icon. Mobile devices use web clip icons when a user wants to add your web application or web page link to their device's Home screen. This problem is similar to the favicon issue because most mobile devices will look for an apple-touch-icon.png file in the root of your application. Its name would have you think only Apple devices look for these icons, but Android devices also look for web clip icons in the root of your application. If a web clip icon isn't there, you'll get a 404 error. The following HTML may be familiar to you:

```
<link rel="apple-touch-icon" href="apple-touch-icon.png">
```

Unfortunately, it gets worse. Some devices will look for different sizes of web clip icons as shown in the next listing.

Listing 10.4 Common web clip icons

```
<link rel="apple-touch-icon-precomposed"
href="apple-touch-icon-precomposed.png">
<link rel="apple-touch-icon-precomposed"
href="apple-touch-icon-72x72-precomposed.png">
<link rel="apple-touch-icon-precomposed"
href="apple-touch-icon-114x114-precomposed.png">
<link rel="apple-touch-icon-precomposed"
href="apple-touch-icon-144x144-precomposed.png">
```

Much like the favicon, you can include these web clip icons in your HTML to make sure devices know where to find them, but you could also ignore the web clip icons in your RouteConfig.cs file.

Listing 10.5 Ignoring web clip icons in the RouteConfig.cs file

```
public class RouteConfig
{
    public static void RegisterRoutes(RouteCollection routes)
    {
        routes.IgnoreRoute("{resource}.axd/{*pathInfo}");

            routes.MapRoute(
            name: "Default",
            url: "{controller}/{action}/{id}",
            defaults: new { controller = "Surf",
                        action = "Index",
                        id = UrlParameter.Optional }
        );

        // Ignore the favicon
        routes.IgnoreRoute("favicon.ico");

        // Ignore web clip icons
        routes.IgnoreRoute("apple-touch-icon-precomposed.png");         <—┐
        routes.IgnoreRoute("apple-touch-icon-72x72-precomposed.png");
        routes.IgnoreRoute("apple-touch-icon-72x72.png");
        routes.IgnoreRoute("apple-touch-icon-57x57-precomposed.png");
        routes.IgnoreRoute("apple-touch-icon-57x57.png");
        routes.IgnoreRoute("apple-touch-icon-144x144-precomposed.png");
        routes.IgnoreRoute("apple-touch-icon-144x144.png");
```

It's best to include every web clip icon size.

```
        routes.IgnoreRoute("apple-touch-icon-114x114-precomposed.png");
        routes.IgnoreRoute("apple-touch-icon-114x114.png");
        routes.IgnoreRoute("apple-touch-icon.png");              ◁┤  There are quite a
    }                                                                few web clip icons!
```

You could choose to include all these types of web clip icons in your application, or you could tell MVC it doesn't need to look for them. Either way, it's important to think about web clip icons because extra lookups might be causing extra disk I/O and computation, all of which adversely affect response times and increase server load.

10.4   *Utilizing a code profiler*

In the first two parts of this book, you have taken an application from a dismally performing front end to a highly optimized one. You may get to a point in your application's development where you're happy with the front-end code's performance, but for some reason the website is still running slowly and the pages are taking longer than they should to load.

This back-end load time may be evident in a waterfall chart of your web page. Figure 10.5 shows a waterfall chart for a web page with a bottleneck occurring in the back-end code.

Diagnosing the problem can be extremely frustrating and you may often find yourself looking in the wrong place. The only way to find the bottlenecks in your back-end code is to use a profiling tool. Many profiling tools are available, and here are a few of the most well-known:

- *DotTrace*—www.jetbrains.com/profiler/
- *ANTS performance profiler*—http://mng.bz/C9kl
- *Telerik JustTrace*—http://mng.bz/ibG3
- *MiniProfiler*—http://miniprofiler.com

One of my favorite ASP.NET MVC profiling tools is MiniProfiler. It's a free download and allows you to profile your MVC application as well as any database queries, Entity Framework queries, Linq2SQL queries, and individual pieces of code.

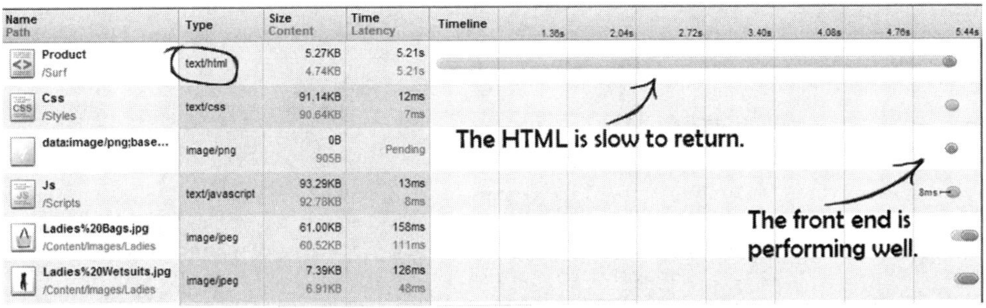

Figure 10.5   A waterfall chart shows that of all the components, the HTML takes the longest to return. This is a good indication that you need to look at the back-end code to improve page load times.

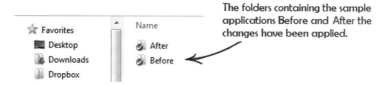

Figure 10.6 The folder structure of each chapter. Each folder will also contain both an ASP.NET MVC version of the application and an ASP.NET Web Forms version.

As you've gone through each chapter, you've improved the Surf Store application's performance step-by-step. When you look at the sample code, you'll notice a folder for almost every chapter in this book. Each folder contains Before and After folders, as you can see in figure 10.6, repeated from chapter 3.

In this chapter, you're going to set up the Surf Store application so we can profile the code with MiniProfiler. The sample code for this chapter has changed slightly because I've updated it to use a local database instead of retrieving the images from disk. As you're focusing on the back-end code in these next chapters, I wanted to get as close to a real-world coding scenario as possible. To create a challenge for the profiler, I purposely injected code to make the website perform slowly when hitting the database.

> **NOTE** It's important to disable HTTP caching and output caching when profiling your website with MiniProfiler. You're looking to identify code bottlenecks and not front-end performance bottlenecks, so it's best to disable them. HTTP caching will only skew the results upon reloading the page. Refer to chapter 4 if you'd like to disable HTTP caching temporarily for your web application.

Let's start profiling. First, we need to add the MiniProfiler library to the sample application by downloading the library from http://miniprofiler.com, or by using the NuGet package manager in Visual Studio 2012. If you aren't familiar with NuGet, it's a free open source package management system for the .NET platform. Instead of searching for an open source library on a website, NuGet contains a list of thousands of free libraries that easily integrate and download into your application. It's very handy because you can quickly add a library to your application without having to visit multiple websites; the libraries are all in one place. Navigate to your Solution Explorer and right-click References. Figure 10.7 shows this in action.

Next, search for MiniProfiler in the search bar and the NuGet package manager will locate the MiniProfiler package for you. Click Install and the required dependencies will be added to your application. Figure 10.8 shows the NuGet package manager and the interface that allows you to easily locate and download the libraries you need to add to your application.

You're almost ready to begin profiling, but first we need to set up a few things. Open the Layout Razor view and add a bit of code that will allow you to see your profiling results. Add the code in listing 10.6 immediately before the closing body tag.

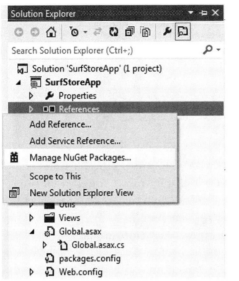

Figure 10.7   Right-click References in the Solution Explorer to add a NuGet package to your application.

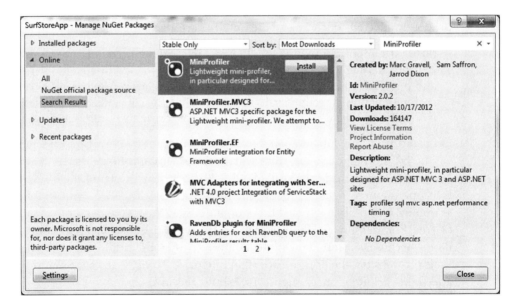

Figure 10.8   The NuGet package manager UI

Listing 10.6   Add UI components to the Layout view

```
@using SurfStoreApp.Utils
@using System.Web.Optimization;
@using StackExchange.Profiling;

<!DOCTYPE html>
<html lang="en">
```

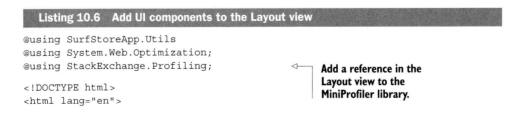

Add a reference in the Layout view to the MiniProfiler library.

```
<head>
    <meta charset="utf-8">
    <title>Surf Store Application</title><link rel="shortcut icon"
    href="@Html.CdnUrl("~/Content/Images/favicon.ico")" />
    <meta name="viewport" content="width=device-width, initial-scale=1.0">
    <meta name="description" content="">
    <meta name="author" content="">
    @Styles.Render("~/Styles/Css")
</head>
<body>

  . . . . . . . . . .

    @RenderBody()
    <hr>
    <footer class="footer">
     <p class="pull-right"><a href="/">Back to top</a></p>
     <p>Surf Store 2012</p>
    </footer>
  </div>
  <!--/.fluid-container-->
  @MiniProfiler.RenderIncludes()
  @Scripts.Render("~/Scripts/Js")
</body></html>
```

> **Writes out the CSS and JavaScript that renders the profiling results.**

The code has been shortened to keep it simple. You're including code that will write out the CSS and JavaScript that will output the profiling results to the web page.

Next, you need to update the Global.asax file and initialize the MiniProfiler so it will start profiling when your application fires up. The next listing contains code you'll need to add to the Global.asax file.

Listing 10.7 Start the profiler in the Global.asax file

```
using StackExchange.Profiling;

namespace SurfStoreApp
{
    public class MvcApplication : System.Web.HttpApplication
    {
      protected void Application_BeginRequest()
      {
       //  Start the MiniProfiler
       if (Request.IsLocal)
       {
        MiniProfiler.Start();
       }
      }

    protected void Application_EndRequest()
    {
      MiniProfiler.Stop();
    }

    protected void Application_Start()
    {
```

> **Add a reference to the MiniProfiler library.**

> **MiniProfiler is designed to run in production code. You can decide whether to hide or show the profiling information with this simple check.**

> **If the HTTP request that executes this code is in a local environment, start the MiniProfiler.**

> **Stop the profiler.**

```
    .....register routes, etc.
    }
}}
```

The code we've added only is executed if the application is running locally. It checks for the presence of a local HTTP request and if true, it starts MiniProfiler. This check is added for security reasons, in case you deployed your application to a production environment with the profiling code still enabled. You wouldn't want anyone to see this sensitive information. It's also worth mentioning that MiniProfiler is designed for production use. A line of code in the previous listing uses `Request.IsLocal` to see if the code is being run in a local environment. As an added security measure, that line of code could just as easily be `User.IsAdmin || Request.IsLocal`.

MiniProfiler allows you to choose the specific parts of your application that you'd like to profile. Instead of profiling the entire application, you can specify a piece of code to profile. It's lightweight and you choose the areas you wish to focus on. The next snippet shows a profiling block wrapped around a piece of code.

```
var profiler = MiniProfiler.Current;
using (profiler.Step("Important code"))
{
    // Some important code goes here
}
```

This code snippet contains a reference to the current instance of MiniProfiler. It is then used in a `using` statement to profile a section of the code. You can have as many of these profiling blocks as you wish, and you can even use them in downstream methods. It's also important to label the profiling block so you know where to pinpoint your code during profiling. Without labels you can easily become lost in the profiling blocks.

A good page to profile in the Surf Store application is the Products page. It's retrieving a list of products based on a category from the database. This bit of code might be inefficient and cause the page to load slowly. Start, as shown in the following listing, by implementing the profiling blocks around the code you wish to examine further.

Listing 10.8 The `Action` on the MVC controller

```
using StackExchange.Profiling;                    ◁─┐  Add a reference to the
                                                     │  MiniProfiler library.
public class SurfController : Controller
{
    public ActionResult Product(string category)
  {
    // Check if a category was passed in first.
    if (!string.IsNullOrWhiteSpace(category))
    {
      List<ProductDetail> productDetails = new List<ProductDetail>();
      var profiler = MiniProfiler.Current;
      // it's ok if this is null
```

```
using (profiler.Step("Retrieve Products"))
{
    // Retrieve the products for the category
    ProductLogic productLogic = new ProductLogic();
    productDetails =
productLogic.GetProductDetailByCategory(category);
}

    // Loop through the results and add to our model
    List<ProductModel> productModel = new List<ProductModel>();
    using (profiler.Step("Build Model"))
    {
        foreach (ProductDetail product in productDetails)
        {
            productModel.Add(new ProductModel
            {
                ImageDescription = product.ProductDescription,
                ImageUrl = product.ImageUrl
            });
        }
    }

    // Return the populated model to the view
    return View(productModel);
}

    // Incorrect parameters were passed in, so return nothing.
    return View();
}
}
```

Wrap a profiling block around individual pieces of code. You can also name the profiling blocks to make them easier to locate at a later stage. This block profiles the image details retrieved from the database.

This profiling block profiles the MVC model created from the image details.

The listing contains the Surf Store application's code that reads a list of images from a database. This code might not be running as efficiently as it should and using Mini-Profiler will give you a chance to identify any inefficient code. Notice that the code contains profiling blocks that are wrapped around methods and individual lines of code. These profiling blocks can be named, which makes it easier to identify the code at a later stage. MiniProfiler will automatically tell you how long it takes for actions to execute and views to render, and the profiling blocks are useful if you wish to investigate specific pieces of code manually.

That's it. You're ready to fire up the application and begin profiling. If you navigate to the Products page of the Surf Store application, you'll notice profiling details in the top-left corner of the screen. Click the ms duration in the corner and you'll be presented with profiling details similar to those in figure 10.9.

In figure 10.9, notice that the profiler also details the full-page lifecycle, so if any intensive JavaScript runs on the front end, you'll be able to identify that, too. The results show the profiling blocks we added in listing 10.8, and you'll notice that the Retrieve Products profiling block took seven seconds to execute. The front-end code seems quite efficient in comparison and took no time at all to respond. Before profiling, I purposely injected a piece of code into the SurfStoreApp.Data project that will block the current thread for around five seconds. Using MiniProfiler helped me to identify where the bottleneck lies.

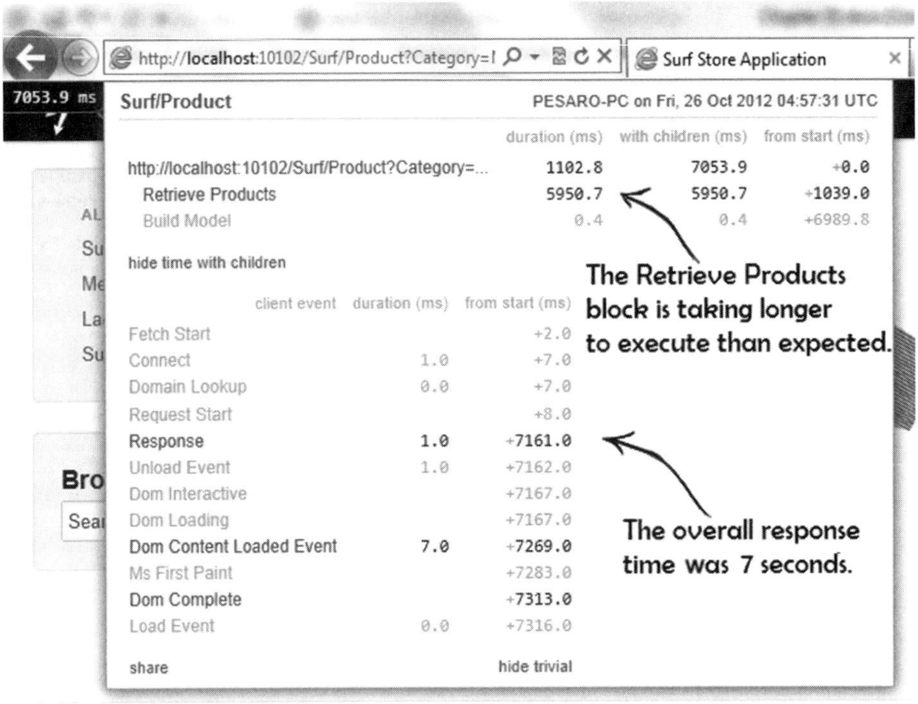

Figure 10.9   MiniProfiler results capture the full page cycle as well as internal code.

After removing the blocking thread, MiniProfiler immediately reflects these changes. Figure 10.10 shows the Retrieve Products profiling block is running a lot quicker now, and your overall page load time has been reduced significantly.

Using MiniProfiler, you were able to identify easily a problem area in the code. The profiling blocks can be chained together and used in downstream methods, so you should be able to drill down continuously until you find the source of the problem in your code. By using a code profiler, you're able to take any guesswork out of your performance issues.

10.4.1   *MiniProfiler for database profiling*

One of the powerful features of MiniProfiler is its ability to profile databases, which can be pretty handy if you need to dig a little deeper into your application. It has built-in support for any kind of `DbConnection`, and it supports Entity Framework and Linq-2-SQL.

There may be a few inefficient queries running on your database, or you may find you're executing the same query multiple times with different parameters. Database profiling quickly allows you to find queries you may be able to batch. The easiest way to use this feature is to use a factory to return your connection, as shown in listing 10.9.

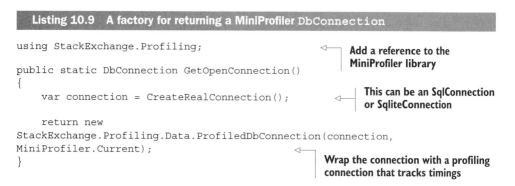

Figure 10.10   MiniProfiler's results after the code update.show improved performance.

Listing 10.9   A factory for returning a MiniProfiler `DbConnection`

```
using StackExchange.Profiling;                    Add a reference to the
                                                  MiniProfiler library
public static DbConnection GetOpenConnection()
{
    var connection = CreateRealConnection();      This can be an SqlConnection
                                                  or SqliteConnection
    return new
StackExchange.Profiling.Data.ProfiledDbConnection(connection,
MiniProfiler.Current);
}                                                 Wrap the connection with a profiling
                                                  connection that tracks timings
```

If you use this connection when querying the database now, you'll find that MiniProfiler will respond and display useful debugging information. Figure 10.11 shows detailed information about a query being executed multiple times.

This detailed information about your SQL queries can be very useful when identifying bottlenecks in your code. It's easy to use the same query twice by mistake, but MiniProfiler has made it easy to pinpoint the issue.

OnActionExecuting	ProfileLinkStats (
T+ 13.6 ms	
DUPLICATE Reader	SELECT count(*) a:
0.4 ms	FROM Posts2Votes \
	JOIN Post:
	WHERE p.DeletionD:
	AND p.PostTyp(
	AND v.Del(
	AND v.Vot(
	AND v.Cre:
	AND v.Use!

OnActionExecuting	ProfileLinkStats (
T+ 14.4 ms	
DUPLICATE Reader	SELECT count(*) a:
0.4 ms	FROM Posts2Votes \
	JOIN Post:
	WHERE p.DeletionD:
	AND p.PostTyp(
	AND v.Del(

Figure 10.11   MiniProfiler results that show duplicate SQL queries being executed.

10.5   Summary

Although 80 to 90% of end user response time is spent on the front end of a website, you may have poorly optimized code running behind the scenes of your application. In this chapter, you shifted focus and looked at different techniques that will enable you to fine-tune your ASP.NET MVC application to squeeze out that last bit of performance.

Often you'll need to closely scrutinize the ASP.NET framework. Many standard out-of-the-box projects might contain unnecessary settings, such as too many view engines, that could add extra overhead to your application.

Running your code in Release mode is a vital part of deploying your application to a production environment. Running your code in Debug mode means your code isn't running at its best. This is okay if you're still developing your website, but it isn't ideal if your website is on a live server. A web application running in Release mode is optimized for performance.

Quite often you'll also need to dive a little deeper into the mechanics of your application and use a profiling tool to identify any bottlenecks. Free tools such as MiniProfiler easily integrate with ASP.NET MVC and can provide useful information that will allow you to pinpoint the exact source of your performance problems.

This chapter provided a good insight into the deeper workings of the ASP.NET MVC framework. By applying these fine-tuning improvements, you can ensure that your MVC application is running at its peak performance. In the next chapter, you'll learn techniques to fine-tune an ASP.NET Web Forms application. You'll also implement the MiniProfiler tool that will help you identify any problem areas in your website.

Tweaking ASP.NET
Web Forms performance

11

This chapter covers

- Improving HTML
- Changing your settings
- Utilizing a code profiler

In the previous chapter, we started looking deeper into the performance of an ASP.NET MVC application. In this chapter, we begin to look at specific techniques for ASP.NET Web Forms performance. (Chapter 10 focused on ASP.NET MVC performance.)

As you've progressed through this book, you've cut the load time of the Surf Store application in half. That is pretty impressive, considering it was all done using front-end optimization techniques. But what happens when you've optimized the front end of your website as much as possible, yet your web pages still load slowly? This is a good indication that you should look at the code that powers the application. Although the performance of a website can be drastically improved by focusing on the front end, there will undoubtedly come a time when a back-end code issue will affect your application.

In this chapter we're going to look at ASP.NET Web Forms-specific techniques that will help improve your page load times as well as the overall performance of your application. Then we'll look at a tool that will help you identify bottlenecks or inefficient code in your application. This profiling tool is different from the tools you've used so far, because it will integrate with the back-end code and pinpoint exact pieces of code that may be causing bottlenecks.

11.1   HTML improvements

A lot of handy features have been built into ASP.NET that make your life as a developer easier. Although these features are great, they don't always generate performance-optimized HTML. In previous versions of ASP.NET, the framework modified the client-side IDs to identify each unique control. This tended to create HTML that left you with the ID of each control that you defined in the markup with something that looks like `"ctl00_MasterPageBody_ctl01_Textbox1"`.

At first sight, this doesn't seem like an issue, but as more nested controls were added to a page, the IDs of these controls became longer. This inevitably led to bloated pages. If you've ever tried to write client-side JavaScript against one of these pages, you'll know the frustration this can cause: each control generated a unique ID at runtime, so you couldn't identify a control until the page was displayed.

Apart from making JavaScript development easier, these HTML improvements also bring another benefit: performance. In chapter 6 you learned a few of the performance benefits HTML5 can bring to your application, reduced page size being one of them. If you have a large and complex web page, making sure the client-side IDs are shorter and easier to identify also reduces overall page weight.

One of the key concepts we've been focusing on in this book is reducing the size of the request a web page makes; this includes the size of the web page itself. Remember, by using less HTML you're also using fewer bytes when a page loads.

In ASP.NET 4.5 Web Forms, every control contains a property called `ClientID-Mode` that selects the behavior of the client-side ID. You have a choice of four possible values:

- `AutoID`—This is the default mode and will generate any client IDs the way that it has in previous versions of ASP.NET. You'll notice client IDs that are similar to `"ctl00_MasterPageBody_ctl01_Textbox1"`.
- `Predictable`—This mode is used when the framework needs to ensure uniqueness in a predictable way. It trims any `"ctl00"` ID strings from the client ID.
- `Static`—This mode puts full control in the developer's hands: it will generate an ID with the name of your choosing.
- `Inherit`—This looks to the control's parent to get its value for `ClientID-Mode`. It tells the control to defer to the parent container control's naming behavior mode.

Let's look at the output the different `ClientIDModes` generate. The following listing shows the markup in Visual Studio before you've rendered the page.

Listing 11.1 Working with `ClientIDMode` in Visual Studio

The ClientIDMode is set to Inherit. This produces a shorter ID, but still includes the parent container control's name.

```
<asp:TextBox ID="TextBox1" ClientIDMode="AutoID"
➥ runat="server" />

<asp:TextBox ID="TextBox2" ClientIDMode="Inherit"
➥ runat="server" />

<asp:TextBox ID="TextBox3" ClientIDMode="Predictable"
➥ runat="server" />

<asp:TextBox ID="TextBox4" ClientIDMode="Static"
➥ runat="server" />
```

Notice the ClientIDMode property on this textbox. AutoID is the default method of generating IDs and it will do so the same way as previous versions of ASP.NET.

Predictable mode is used when the framework must make sure the string is unique. It will keep the parent container control's name.

The ClientIDMode is set to Static. This mode puts the control in your hands and makes sure the naming is exactly as you want it.

As you can see from the code, changing how you render the textbox ID is easy. The HTML in listing 11.1 will render and display like the HTML in figure 11.1.

In figure 11.1, the textbox with the shortest and easiest to understand ID is TextBox4, which was generated with a `Static ClientIDMode`. Notice the name property on the textbox is still a lot longer than it needs to be. Unfortunately, this is built into ASP.NET Web Forms and it isn't a good idea to remove it. ASP.NET uses the name property to locate the `Postback` control and to route `Postback` data and events.

As it stands, you've managed to reduce the length and simplify the ID of a server-side control. Apart from making it a lot easier to read the control's ID, you have also reduced the number of bytes on the web page.

I know this may seem like a trivial amount, but it can add up if you have a lot of server-side controls on a web page. I took a popular e-commerce website that uses ASP.NET Web Forms, looked at the HTML from a standard product display page, and compared the results before and after shortening the client IDs. The original page weight was 163 KB; it was reduced to 137 KB once the updates were made. Shortening the names of the input fields saved 26 KB. I changed nothing else!

Making changes to existing HTML sounds easy in theory, but it's a lot harder in practice because there can be loads of dependencies to the controls' IDs. If you're about to embark on a new project, do it the right way from the start. If you're developing new areas on an existing site, remember that the weight of the client IDs can quickly add up.

```
<input name="ctl00$MainContent$TextBox1" type="text" id="ctl00_MainContent_TextBox1" />

<input name="ctl00$MainContent$TextBox2" type="text" id="MainContent_TextBox2" />

<input name="ctl00$MainContent$TextBox3" type="text" id="MainContent_TextBox3" />

<input name="ctl00$MainContent$TextBox4" type="text" id="TextBox4" />
```

Figure 11.1 Generating different IDs with ClientIDMode on an ASP.NET control

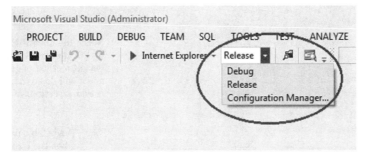

Figure 11.2   Visual Studio allows you to publish your code in two different modes: Debug and Release.

11.2   *Web.config settings*

There are a few simple changes you can make in the Web.config file of your ASP.NET Web Forms application. A wide range of settings can be finely tuned and tweaked in the Web.config file to improve the performance of your application. Knowing when and where to apply these changes is what's important.

11.2.1   *Publishing your application in Release mode*

If you are about to deploy your website, one of the most important things you can do is make sure it's been compiled and deployed in Release mode. You may be familiar with the Configuration Manager drop-down available in Visual Studio, shown in figure 11.2 and repeated from chapter 10.

As the name states, Debug mode is for debugging and is meant to make your life as a developer a lot easier. Visual Studio's built-in debugger allows you to pause and step through code in order to debug and visualize the values in your application. Unfortunately, Debug mode isn't ideal for code performance. When your code is running in Debug mode a number of nonoptimal things are happening:

- Code executes more slowly because additional debug paths are enabled.
- Much more memory is used by the application at runtime.
- Certain timeouts are disabled, so you're blind to any long-running operations that should have timed out.
- The bundling and minification code you wrote in chapter 5 won't be enabled because it runs in Release mode.

A quick way to see if your application is running in Debug mode is to look at the Web.config file. You might notice something similar to the next listing.

> **Listing 11.2   A Web.config file with `debug=true` attribute**

```
<system.web>
 <compilation debug="true" targetFramework="4.5" />
 <httpRuntime targetFramework="4.5" />
```
◁─┤ **Indicates the code is running in Debug mode.**

```
<pages>
  <namespaces>
    <add namespace="System.Web.Optimization" />
  </namespaces>
  <controls>
    <add assembly="Microsoft.AspNet.Web.Optimization.WebForms"
➥      namespace="Microsoft.AspNet.Web.Optimization.WebForms"
                  tagPrefix="webopt" />
  </controls>
</pages>
</system.web>
```

The listing contains a snippet of settings from a typical ASP.NET Web Forms Web.config file. The debug=true setting indicates the code is running in Debug mode. It's not ideal for your application to be running in Debug mode in a production environment. The preferred way to switch to Release mode is to deploy your application using Visual Studio and publish in Release mode. You can also remove debug=true from your Web.config or replace it with debug=false. The application pool in IIS will recycle and the application will then run in Release mode.

This setting is important! If you're running your application in a production environment in Debug mode, it's almost definitely running slower than necessary, so make sure you publish your application in Release mode.

11.2.2 *Disable tracing if it's not used*

Tracing is a great feature that's been built into the ASP.NET framework. It enables you to track the diagnostics of an application to the page's output by sending information to the requesting browser. Optionally, you can view this information from a separate trace viewer that displays trace information for every page in an ASP.NET web application. Tracing comes in handy when you need to investigate unwanted errors or results while ASP.NET processes a page request, but you'll pay a price.

Tracing adds performance overhead and might expose private information, so you should enable it only while an application is being analyzed.

To disable tracing, turn it off in your Web.config file. The code in the next listing shows how simple it is to disable tracing in your application.

Listing 11.3 Disabling tracing in Web.config

```
<system.web>
  <compilation debug="true" targetFramework="4.5" />
  <!-- Disable Tracing -->
  <trace enabled="false" requestLimit="10" pageOutput="false" />    ◁─┐
  <httpRuntime targetFramework="4.5" />
. . . .                              Set enabled=false on the
</system.web>                      <trace> tag to disable tracing.
```

After setting enabled=false on the <trace> tag, you won't be affected by the negative performance hits that tracing can cause.

11.2.3 *Disable session state*

A handy built-in feature of the ASP.NET framework is session state which allows you to store and retrieve values into a session for a user. As the user navigates through the pages in your web application, you can easily retrieve these values from the session. This feature is handy because HTTP is a stateless protocol, meaning a web server treats each HTTP request for a page as an independent request. By default, the server retains no knowledge of variable values used during previous requests. You may find yourself in a situation where it's necessary to store certain values for the duration of a user's session. I personally have a bit of a love/hate relationship with this feature. It's useful, but you can find yourself dumping values into the session state unnecessarily, causing it to become bloated.

ASP.NET session state is enabled by default for all ASP.NET applications. Although this is useful and you can start using it right away, you'll pay the price in memory, even if you don't use it. Session state requires memory to store the values and it can also be time consuming when you store or retrieve values from memory.

You can disable session state in your application in a number of ways. If you aren't using session state on certain pages, you can and should disable it on your web form with the following code:

```
<%@ Page EnableSessionState="False" . . . . . %>
```

You may also find yourself in a situation where you may be reading from session state, but not writing to it. You can also set session state to ReadOnly, shown in the following code:

```
<%@ Page EnableSessionState="ReadOnly" . . . . . %>
```

The preceding code sets the session state for a page to ReadOnly, but if you aren't using session state, you may want to disable it across the entire application. You can disable it easily in your Web.config file:

```
<sessionState mode="Off" />
```

Minimizing the use of session state increases the overall performance of your application, particularly under high traffic. Although it may not increase the load time of a web page immediately, it will definitely improve the health of your application as a whole.

11.2.4 *Disable ViewState when it's not needed*

ViewState is a technique used by an ASP.NET web page to persist changes to the state of a Web Form across Postbacks. The ASP.NET framework will encode a serialized object as a binary Base64-encoded string and add it to the page. The HTML in the next listing might look familiar.

Listing 11.4   ViewState inside an HTML page

```
<form method="post" action="./" id="SearchSubmit">
  <div class="aspNetHidden">
  <input type="hidden" name="VIEWSTATE" id="VIEWSTATE"
➡️        value="KM5WEgrkiFRaM24e4FVPXchpZmHIOyncVAz7s+47/
➡️        Yu7Ou5P8KLvQuQUeYoaZ0VkubS0232pl7dWPZxeZHQOg+Mk
➡️        L6m63RooXh/0AU+wKoA=" />
  </div>
. . . . . . </form>
```

A hidden field is added to the web application with a Base64-encoded string. This hidden field is used to persist state across Postbacks.

The HTML markup in the listing shows how a hidden field is added to each page in a web application. This technique has been around since the early days of ASP.NET and continues to be a powerful and simple way to persist small pieces of data. ViewState allows state to be persisted with the client and it doesn't require cookies or server memory to save this state. However, the Base64-encoded string that is included in a web page can sometimes add an overhead of about 30 percent to your web pages. The time it takes for the object to get serialized also comes at a small cost.

ASP.NET ViewState is an important part of maintaining state in your application. Without it, certain pages and controls on your website won't function properly. Proceed cautiously and disable it only when it's absolutely not needed.

A page that might not need ViewState might be one that displays information and does not post back to itself. To disable ViewState, include the following code in your page directive:

```
<%@ Page EnableViewState="false" . . . . %>
```

Disabling ViewState on pages that don't need it improves the performance of those pages significantly. The extra data added to the page will also add to the weight of the HTML returned from the server, and by removing it, you're making sure your web page stays light.

11.3   *Response.Redirect vs. Server.Transfer*

In chapter 2 we discussed the HTTP response codes a server can return to the browser. When you use `Response.Redirect()` in your code to redirect a user between pages on your website, a 302 HTTP response code is returned from the server. A 302 HTTP status code indicates to the browser that it should perform a temporary redirect. A `Response.Redirect()` will send you to a new page and update the address bar with the new page. Unfortunately, `Response.Redirect()` sends an extra request to the server, which could be avoided.

An option is to use `Server.Transfer()` instead. `Server.Transfer()` helps reduce server requests because it happens without the browser knowing anything. When the browser requests a web page, the content of another page is returned. Instead of telling the browser to redirect, it changes the focus on the web server and transfers the request. You don't get as many HTTP requests coming through, which eases the pressure on your web server and makes your applications run faster.

With different methods come different challenges. Using `Server.Transfer()` doesn't change the URL in the address bar of the browser. This can be quite confusing during debugging, and because the URL doesn't change, a user might bookmark the wrong page. You also can't use `Server.Transfer()` to redirect to a page on an external site, it will only redirect within the same application.

If used in the right circumstances, `Server.Transfer()` can be quite powerful and will reduce the number of HTTP requests coming to and from your server. This will definitely lighten the load on your server and improve the overall performance of your web application.

11.4   *Utilizing a code profiler*

In parts 1 and 2, we concentrated solely on front-end performance and improving the page load times in a web application. In those chapters, you learned that the biggest gains in terms of page load times can be made on the front end because the changes are scalable, easy to implement, and relatively fast—wait time is how long it takes for the components in a page to download. You took an ASP.NET Web Forms application from a dismal page load time to a speedy, high-performance load time.

But what happens when you've optimized the front end of your website as much as possible, but you still experience a long delay when waiting for the page to load? It may be time to take a closer look at your website's back-end code. Figure 11.3 shows a waterfall chart for a web page with a bottleneck in the back-end code.

Trying to diagnose the bottleneck can be extremely frustrating and you may find yourself looking in the wrong place. The only way to find the bottlenecks in your back-end code is to use a profiling tool. There are many profiling tools that will help you profile and locate the source of your performance issue or memory leak.

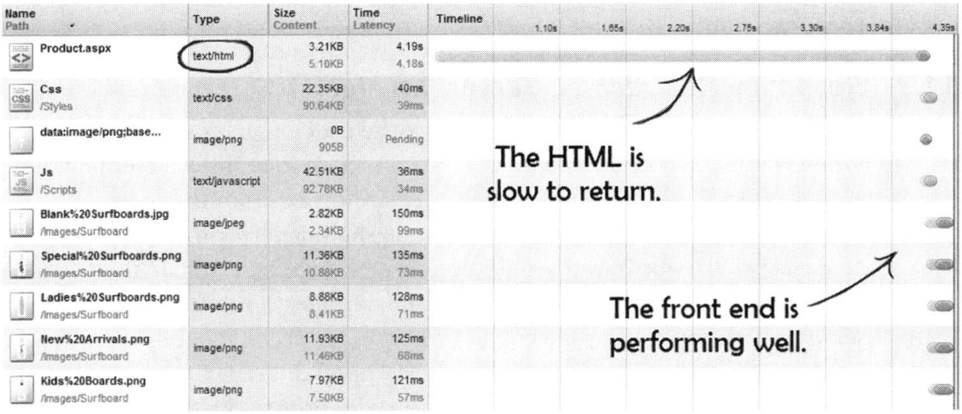

Figure 11.3   A waterfall chart shows that of all the components, the HTML takes the longest to return. This is an indication that you need to look at the back-end code to improve page load times.

These are a few of the better-known tools:

- *DotTrace*—www.jetbrains.com/profiler/
- *ANTS performance profiler*—http://mng.bz/C9kl
- *Telerik JustTrace*—http://mng.bz/ibG3
- *MiniProfiler*—http://miniprofiler.com

One of my favorite tools to use when profiling an ASP.NET website is the MiniProfiler tool. In chapter 10, you saw how it can be used to profile an ASP.NET MVC application. The tool is flexible and built to be used against ASP.NET Web Forms applications, too. It's a free download and allows you to profile your Web Forms application as well as any database queries, Entity Framework queries, Linq2SQL queries, and individual pieces of code.

In this chapter, you're going to set up the Surf Store application so you can profile the code with MiniProfiler. The sample code for this chapter is located in the chapter 11 folder. The code for chapter 11 has changed slightly because I've updated the sample application to use a local database instead of retrieving the images from disk. As you're focusing on the back-end code now, I wanted to get as close to a real-world scenario as possible. To create a challenge for the profiler, I purposely injected code to make the website perform slowly when hitting the database.

Let's start profiling. First, you need to add the MiniProfiler library to the sample application. You can download the library from miniprofiler.com, or by using the NuGet package manager in Visual Studio 2012. NuGet is a free, open source package management system for the .NET platform. Instead of searching for an open source library on a website, NuGet contains a list of thousands of free libraries that easily integrate and download into your application. It's handy because it allows you to add a library to your application without having to visit multiple websites; the libraries are all in one place and are easily searchable. Navigate to your Solution Explorer and right-click References. Next, click Manage NuGet Packages. Figure 11.4 shows this in action.

Next, search for MiniProfiler in the search bar and the NuGet package manager will locate the MiniProfiler package for you. Click Install and the required dependencies will be added to your application. Figure 11.5 shows the NuGet package manager and the interface that allows you to easily locate and download the libraries you want to add to your application.

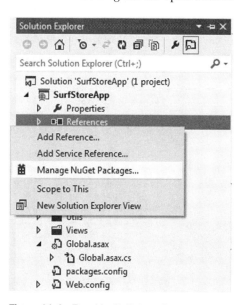

Figure 11.4   To add a NuGet package to your application, right-click References in the Solution Explorer.

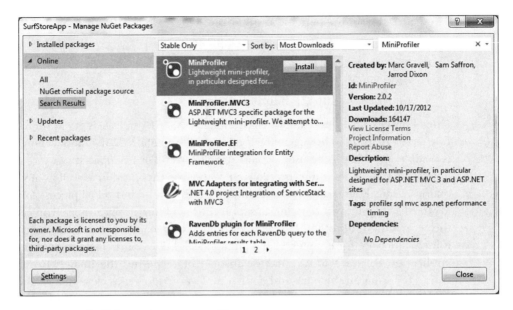

Figure 11.5   The NuGet package manager UI

Open the Master page and add a piece of code that allows you to see the code profile results. Add the code in the next listing to the <head> tag of your HTML.

Listing 11.5   Add UI components to the Master page

```
<%@ Import Namespace="SurfStoreApp.Utils" %>

<!DOCTYPE html>
<html lang="en">
<head>
 <asp:ContentPlaceHolder runat="server" ID="HeadContent">
     <meta charset="utf-8">
     <title>Surf Store Application</title>
     <link rel="shortcut icon"
href="<%=
FileVersionUtils.BuildVersionedFileName("Images/favicon.ico") %>" />
     <meta name="viewport" content="width=device-width, initial-scale=1.0">
     <meta name="description" content="">
     <meta name="author" content="">
     <%= Styles.Render("~/Styles/Css")%>
     <%= StackExchange.Profiling.MiniProfiler.RenderIncludes() %>        ◁─┐
 </asp:ContentPlaceHolder>
</head>
<body>

. . . . . .

<body>
</html>
```

Add the code that will write out
the CSS and JavaScript required
to render the profiling results.

The example has been shortened to keep it simple, but you're including code that will write out the CSS and JavaScript required to output the profiling results to the web page.

Now you need to update the Global.asax file and initialize the MiniProfiler so it starts profiling when your application fires up. This listing shows the code you need to add to the Global.asax file.

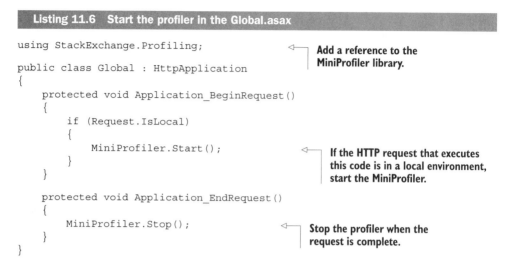

Listing 11.6 Start the profiler in the Global.asax

```
using StackExchange.Profiling;                    Add a reference to the
                                                  MiniProfiler library.
public class Global : HttpApplication
{
    protected void Application_BeginRequest()
    {
        if (Request.IsLocal)
        {
            MiniProfiler.Start();                 If the HTTP request that executes
        }                                         this code is in a local environment,
    }                                             start the MiniProfiler.

    protected void Application_EndRequest()
    {
        MiniProfiler.Stop();                      Stop the profiler when the
    }                                             request is complete.
}
```

The code you've added makes sure the profiler is executed only if the application is running locally. If it detects a local HTTP request, it starts the MiniProfiler. This check is added for security reasons, in case you deployed your application to a production environment with the profiling code still enabled; you wouldn't want anyone to see this sensitive information.

MiniProfiler is lightweight and lets you choose which parts of your application you'd like to profile. Instead of profiling the entire application, you can profile a particular piece of code. The following code snippet shows a profiling block wrapped around a piece of code.

```
var profiler = MiniProfiler.Current;
using (profiler.Step("Important code"))
{
    // Some important code goes here
}
```

The code snippet contains a reference to the current instance of the MiniProfiler. It's then implemented in a using statement to profile a section of the code. You can have as many of these profiling blocks as you wish, and you can even use them in downstream methods. It's also important to label the profiling block so you know where to point your code during profiling. Without labels you can easily become lost in the numerous profiling blocks!

With regards to the Surf Store application, a good page to profile would be the Products page. It's retrieving a list of products based on a category from the database. This bit of code might be inefficient and cause the page to load slowly. Start by implementing the profiling blocks around the code you wish to examine further.

Listing 11.7   Profiling the Product.aspx page

```
using StackExchange.Profiling;                    ◁───  Add a reference to the
                                                         MiniProfiler library.
public partial class Product : System.Web.UI.Page
{
    protected void Page_Load(object sender, EventArgs e)
    {
     // Get the category from the querystring
     string category = Request.QueryString["category"];

     // Check if we received a category
     if (!string.IsNullOrWhiteSpace(category))
     {
         // Display the images
         List<ProductDetail> productsForCategory =
                      new List<ProductDetail>();
         var profiler = MiniProfiler.Current;              ◁──
         using (profiler.Step("Retrieve Products"))
         {
             ProductLogic productLogic = new ProductLogic();
             productsForCategory =
         productLogic.GetProductDetailByCategory(category);
         }

         using (profiler.Step("Build HTML"))               ◁───
         {
             // Loop through each product and build the HTML that
             // we are going to return to the web page
             foreach (ProductDetail product in productsForCategory)
             {
                phProductImages.Controls.Add(
                             BuildHtml(category,
                             product.ImageUrl,
                             product.ProductDescription));
             }
         }
      }
    }
}
```

Wrap a profiling block around individual pieces of code. You can also name the profiling blocks to make them easier to identify and come back to at a later stage. This block profiles image details being retrieved from the database.

This block profiles the creation of the HTML that displays the images.

The sample code is from the Surf Store application that reads a list of images from a database. It might not be running as efficiently as it should, and the MiniProfiler will help you identify any inefficient code. You'll notice the code in the previous listing contains profiling blocks that are wrapped around methods and individual lines of code. They're particularly useful if you want to manually investigate specific pieces of code. MiniProfiler will automatically tell you how long it takes for actions to execute and views to render.

That's it. You're now ready to fire up the application and begin profiling. If we navigate to the Products page of the Surf Store application, you'll notice profiling details in the top-left corner of the screen. Click the millisecond duration message in the upper-left corner and you'll see MiniProfiler profiling details (figure 11.6).

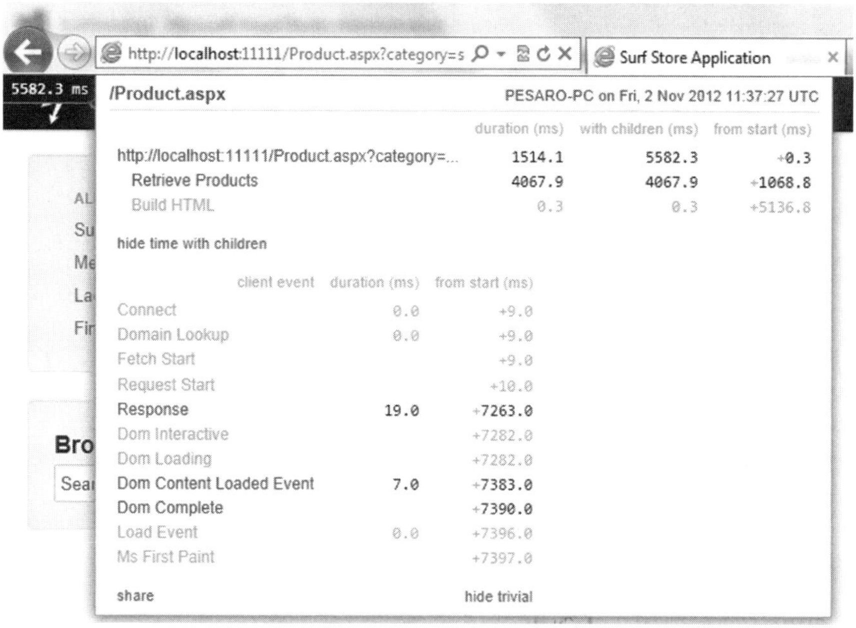

Figure 11.6 MiniProfiler results. They capture the full page cycle as well as internal code.

Notice how the profiler also details the complete page lifecycle, so if any intensive JavaScript runs on the front end, you'll be able to identify that, too. The results also show the profiling blocks we added in listing 11.7.

You'll notice in figure 11.6 that the Retrieve Products profiling block took over four seconds to execute. The front-end code is quite efficient in comparison and took no time at all to respond. Before starting the profiling, I purposely injected a piece of code in the SurfStoreApp.Data project that will block the current thread for about five seconds.

If you concentrate on this bottleneck and improve any inefficient code, you should be able to improve the page load time considerably.

> **NOTE** It's important to disable HTTP caching and output caching when you profile your website with MiniProfiler. You want to identify back-end code bottlenecks, not front-end performance bottlenecks. HTTP caching will only skew the results when you reload the page!

After you remove the inefficient code, MiniProfiler immediately reflects these changes. Figure 11.7 shows how the Retrieve Products profiling block is running a lot quicker now, and your overall page load time has been reduced significantly.

You were able to identify a problem area in the code easily with MiniProfiler. The profiling blocks can be chained together and used in downstream methods, so you should be able to drill down until you find the source of your code problems. By using a code profiler, you're able to take any guesswork out of your performance issues.

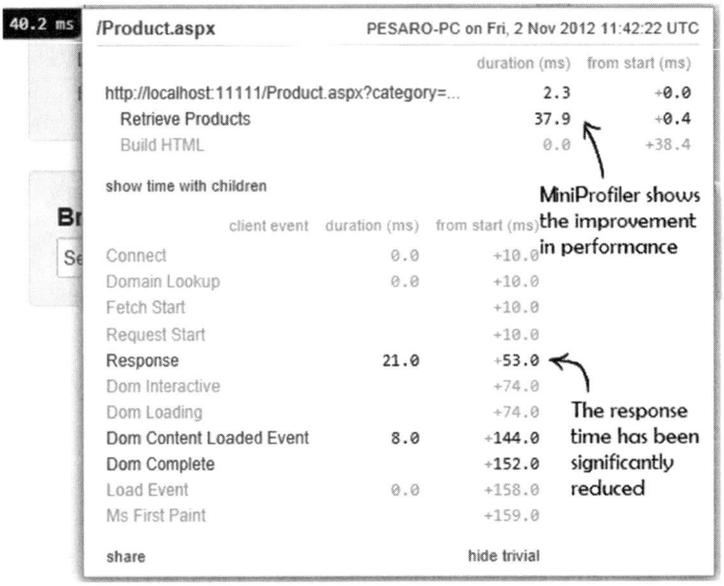

Figure 11.7   MiniProfiler results after the code update

11.5   *Fixing the issue*

The most important part of finding your website's code bottlenecks is being able to fix the problem. Using a profiler allows you to narrow the list of possibilities and identify the root cause of the bottlenecks, but it doesn't show you how to fix them.

Each performance issue requires its own solution. Because of the breadth of issues developers face, you'll be required to call on your own problem-solving skills and expertise.

In this book, I've concentrated on front-end performance issues and given you the tools to identify problem code in your application. The best way to fix an issue buried deep in code is to keep going back to the performance cycle. It may seem like an overwhelming task, but the process of improving your website's load times and performance can be broken down into four key stages. The performance cycle is a summary of the entire website improvement process. Its four stages are a guide to a process which can be applied to any website, regardless of the specific rules and techniques you'll apply, helping you realize performance potential and faster load times.

As you go through the four key stages of the performance cycle, you'll notice the improvement each adjustment to your code will make. Experimenting with different code techniques is often the best way to improve a slow running part of your website. You'll be able to easily decide if you're heading in the right or wrong direction by monitoring and tracking for any signs of change.

11.6 *Summary*

In this chapter you shifted your focus toward the back-end code of a web application. In the first two parts of this book we concentrated on the front-end performance of web applications, but there may come a time when your application runs slower than expected even after you've performed front-end optimization.

By default, ASP.NET Web Forms projects created in Visual Studio are not optimized for performance. A lot of features enabled by default might not be necessary and could cause extra overhead in your application. Since ASP.NET 4, there have been HTML improvements that allow you to provide cleaner HTML that will reduce the overall weight of your web pages.

This chapter highlighted the importance of publishing your applications in Release mode. If your web application is running in Debug mode, your code will execute slower and your application will use more memory. When you deploy your site to a production environment, make sure it's running in Release mode.

We investigated different settings in the Web.config file and examined the pros and cons of disabling certain features to improve performance. Under the correct circumstances, disabling tracing, session state, or ViewState can speed up your application's page load times significantly. By fine-tuning certain settings, you can make sure your Web Forms application is running at its peak performance.

When looking to optimize your back-end code, you will often need to go one step further and use a profiling tool to pinpoint exact bottlenecks in your code. Implementing tools such as MiniProfiler will allow you to profile your code and identify any performance issues.

This free tool integrates easily with ASP.NET Web Forms and can provide you with useful information that will allow you to pinpoint the exact source of your performance problem.

In the next and final chapter of this book, we take a look at object caching. It involves caching frequently used data in order to speed up your application's page load times.

Data caching

This chapter covers

- System.Runtime.Caching
- What should I cache?
- Notes on distributed caching

In the same way that you might keep milk in your fridge until it reaches its expiration date, as I said in chapter 4, browsers can cache information about a website for a set duration of time. When your milk is old, you buy new. After data expires, a browser will fetch the updated version. Much like caching data on a user's browser with HTTP caching, as discussed in chapter 4, you can do the same thing with frequently used information on the server. By caching data on the server, you can easily store information retrieved from the database, or perhaps even an expensive method.

Data caching is the process of storing frequently used data on the server to fulfill subsequent requests. If some data doesn't change often, store it on the server so you don't have to make an expensive call to the database the next time you request it.

Data caching is one of my favorite server-side techniques for speeding up an application and making it more robust. The .NET Framework has great built-in support for data caching and it can be applied to a web application in no time at all.

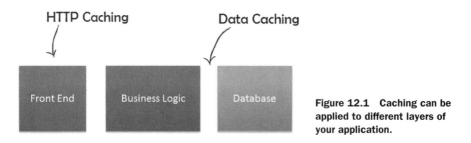

Figure 12.1 **Caching can be applied to different layers of your application.**

This chapter runs through setting up data caching in a web application and shows how easy it is to use this great feature.

12.1   Server-side data caching

This may be the final chapter in this book, but it covers one of the most important aspects of the performance of a web application: server-side data caching. Most applications on the web will work with frequently used data that isn't updated all that often. This makes it a prime candidate for data caching. For example, you may retrieve a list of country names from the database that doesn't change often, or you may retrieve a list of default settings that only changes once every six months. These chunks of data are perfect candidates for data caching, and you can speed up your application considerably by adding them into a cache.

Figure 12.1 shows caching can be applied to layers in the application. If used effectively in each layer in your application, caching can make your application extremely fast.

Fortunately, caching doesn't extend only to databases. You could cache the result of a call to a web service or even a long-running code calculation. If code is called frequently but the returned result doesn't change often, it's ideal for caching. Because the data is retrieved from memory, it's often returned instantly.

12.2   System.Runtime.Caching

The .NET Framework has a built-in set of classes that fall under the System.Runtime.Caching namespace. This namespace contains types that let you implement an in-memory cache in your .NET Framework applications. The cache object enables you to store everything from simple name/value pairs to more complex objects, such as datasets and entire web pages. The classes are also extensible and if you're looking for more flexibility, they allow you to create custom caching providers. The built-in classes that fall under the System.Runtime.Caching namespace are easy to implement and can produce impressive results.

You've been working with the Surf Store application throughout this book. Now you will learn how easy it is to add caching to any ASP.NET application and improve its web page load times. To get started, you need to add a reference to the System.Runtime.Caching library in your project.

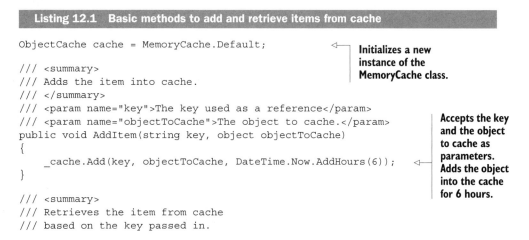

Figure 12.2 A reference to System.Runtime.Caching added to your application

In figure 12.2, a reference to the System.Runtime.Caching namespace is added to start caching in the sample application. Because you're going to add caching in the sample application's data layer, I've added the reference to the SurfStoreApp.Data project.

A few simple methods like the ones shown in the next listing are enough to get started caching.

Listing 12.1 Basic methods to add and retrieve items from cache

```
ObjectCache cache = MemoryCache.Default;          Initializes a new
                                                  instance of the
/// <summary>                                      MemoryCache class.
/// Adds the item into cache.
/// </summary>
/// <param name="key">The key used as a reference</param>
/// <param name="objectToCache">The object to cache.</param>     Accepts the key
public void AddItem(string key, object objectToCache)            and the object
{                                                               to cache as
    _cache.Add(key, objectToCache, DateTime.Now.AddHours(6));    parameters.
}                                                               Adds the object
                                                                into the cache
/// <summary>                                                   for 6 hours.
/// Retrieves the item from cache
/// based on the key passed in.
```

```
/// </summary>
/// <param name="key">The key.</param>
/// <returns></returns>
public object RetrieveItem(string key)
{
    object objectRetrievedFromCache = cache.Get(key);

    return objectRetrievedFromCache;
}
```

Retrieves the object from cache based on the passed in key.

The first line initializes a new instance of the `MemoryCache` class, and you reference to the default `MemoryCache` instance. The `MemoryCache` object is flexible and allows multiple instances inside a single application.

A method allows you to add an item into cache with a key, which you use to retrieve the object from cache when required. It's worth mentioning that `MemoryCache` is not as strict as dictionary-based collections; if you request an item key that doesn't exist, you'll get a null rather than a runtime error.

When you're building your application, you might come across a scenario in which similar objects have similar names. If that happens, consider building a dynamic key string to identify your objects. If you try to add an object into the cache and a key with the same name already exists, the new object will overwrite the older one.

The code in the previous listing is effective, but it could be rewritten so it's easier to reuse and so it takes a dynamic key into account. The following listing is a more effective data caching class you can use throughout your application.

Listing 12.2 Adding and retrieving items from cache

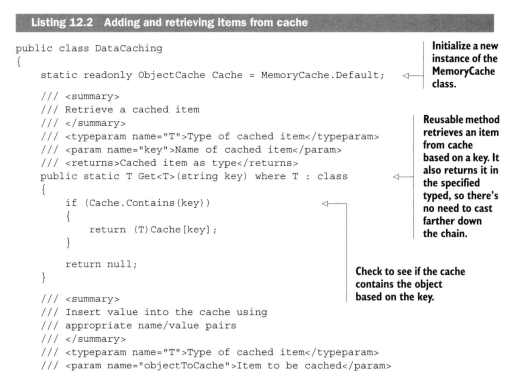

```
public class DataCaching
{
    static readonly ObjectCache Cache = MemoryCache.Default;

    /// <summary>
    /// Retrieve a cached item
    /// </summary>
    /// <typeparam name="T">Type of cached item</typeparam>
    /// <param name="key">Name of cached item</param>
    /// <returns>Cached item as type</returns>
    public static T Get<T>(string key) where T : class
    {
        if (Cache.Contains(key))
        {
            return (T)Cache[key];
        }

        return null;
    }

    /// <summary>
    /// Insert value into the cache using
    /// appropriate name/value pairs
    /// </summary>
    /// <typeparam name="T">Type of cached item</typeparam>
    /// <param name="objectToCache">Item to be cached</param>
```

Initialize a new instance of the MemoryCache class.

Reusable method retrieves an item from cache based on a key. It also returns it in the specified typed, so there's no need to cast farther down the chain.

Check to see if the cache contains the object based on the key.

```
/// <param name="key">Name of item</param>
public static void Add<T>(T objectToCache, string key) where T : class
{
    Cache.Add(key, objectToCache, DateTime.Now.AddDays(30));
}

/// <summary>
/// Remove item from cache
/// </summary>
/// <param name="key">Name of cached item</param>
public static void Clear(string key)
{
    Cache.Remove(key);
}

/// <summary>
/// Gets all cached items as a list by their key.
/// </summary>
/// <returns></returns>
public static List<string> GetAll()
{
    return Cache.Select(keyValuePair => keyValuePair.Key).ToList();
}
}
```

Use this to add an object into the cache. The hardcoded value is 30 days, but you can change that value in your own application.

Remove the item from cache based on the key.

Return a list of all the items in cache.

This code can be used throughout your application to cache data and retrieve different object types from cache. It contains a set of useful dynamic methods and should cover the basic caching needs of an application.

12.3 *What should I cache?*

You can easily store the results of any expensive or long-running operations that aren't likely to change in memory, so they can be retrieved at a later time. The kinds of data you would store in memory might include

- Database lookups
- Expensive calculations that are done in code
- The data from any I/O read (XML file, text file, and so on)
- The result of a web service call

In chapter 4 you investigated HTTP caching and the flexibility of IIS for storing data that doesn't change often in the client's browser. Remember, if data is cached it's refreshed only after it expires. Bear this in mind when designing your application, because caching data that changes frequently can cause headaches when you're debugging your application.

12.4 *The sample application*

In this chapter, you're going to apply caching to the Surf Store application you've been optimizing throughout this book. The Products page of the sample application retrieves product information from the database to display on the Products page. This information doesn't change often and is a prime candidate for data caching.

I've chosen to add caching in the project's Logic layer. You could easily choose to add caching in the Data layer if the GetProductDetailByCategory method is reused frequently. By adding the caching on the Data layer, it will allow you to share the cached information with other methods in the application. The following listing shows the code in action.

Listing 12.3 Using the cache in the sample application

```
public class ProductLogic
{
    /// <summary>                                      Build a dynamic key
    /// Gets the product detail by category.           you can use to store
    /// </summary>                                     the object against.
    /// <param name="category">The category.</param>
    /// <returns></returns>
    public List<ProductDetail> GetProductDetailByCategory(string category)
    {
        // Build a cacheKey
        string cacheKey = "GetProductDetailByCategory-" + category;

        // Try and retrieve the data from the cache            Use the key to retrieve
        List<ProductDetail> productDetails =  DataCaching         the object from cache.
  .Get<List<ProductDetail>>(cacheKey);

        if (productDetails == null)                        Check if the object isn't
        {                                                  in cache and is null.
            // Retrieve from the database
            ProductData productData = new ProductData();      If no objects are in
            productDetails = productData                       cache, retrieve the data
  .GetProductDetailByCategory(category);                       from the database.

            // Add into cache
            DataCaching.Add(productDetails, cacheKey);      Add the data from
        }                                                  the database into
                                                           cache for next time.
        return productDetails;
    }                                          Return the result.
}
```

The code builds a dynamic key that caches the data and retrieves it at a later stage. Because the key is based on the passed-in category and the method name, it should be unique every time.

Look in the cache with the cache key to see if any data is associated to that key. If there's nothing, retrieve the data from the database and add it into cache so it can be retrieved from cache next time.

If the key does find something in cache, return the cached data instead of going to the database. Retrieving the data from cache instead of making a call to the database is significantly faster because you're retrieving directly from memory in the application. This technique can be applied throughout your application to any long-running operations that take place during execution.

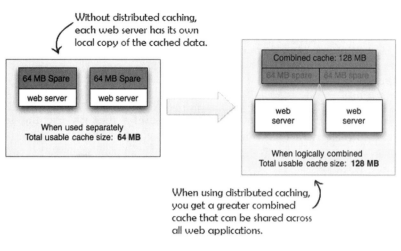

Figure 12.3 Distributed caching across multiple web servers versus caching on individual web servers

12.5 *Notes on distributed caching*

If you run your application in a load-balanced environment with multiple servers, you may need to assess the way you cache your data. In this chapter's example code, all the data in the cache will be stored within the application itself. If your application is running across multiple servers, you'd have a near duplicate copy of the cached data on each server. This can become a problem on your server if the memory grows quite large or if the cached data on each server is out of sync.

To avoid these pitfalls consider using distributed caching instead. Distributed caching allows the cache to span multiple servers so it can grow in size and in transactional capacity.

In figure 12.3, the left side shows how each web server has its own individual copy of the cache. The right side shows the distributed cache with a combined cache. Both servers retrieve data from the same cache instead of accessing their own individual cache. Your servers are more efficient when storing data this way because they're sharing the combined cache. A distributed cache also provides high availability and scalability. If either of the web servers goes down, you'll still have the cached data available for the other web servers.

Distributed caching options available today include

- *Windows Azure Caching*—www.windowsazure.com/en-us/services/caching/
- *Memcached*—memcached.org
- *NCache*—www.alachisoft.com/ncache/
- *Redis*—http://redis.io/

Most of these distributed caching solutions work in a similar way to the System.Runtime .Caching namespace. They allow you to store a chunk of data using a simple key/value pair that can easily be retrieved at a later stage.

If you're looking to grow your application and make sure it's scalable and performing efficiently, consider distributed caching as an alternative to the standard caching in the System.Runtime.Caching namespace.

12.6   *Summary*

In this chapter you learned about in-memory caching in the .NET Framework. The System.Runtime.Caching namespace provides a useful tool for caching frequently accessed data. Instead of continually executing expensive I/O operations, the data returned from these operations can be stored in a cache that allows you to instantly retrieve the data. This cache can be used for common operations such as database lookups and expensive calculations, or for accessing data from a simple I/O read. Using caching in your application will make sure it's scalable as well as extremely fast.

You also briefly investigated implementing a distributed cache if you're running your application across multiple servers. Distributed cache can be an effective way to make sure your application performs at its best if it spans multiple web servers.

12.7   *Look at how far you've come!*

You've completed the final chapter in this book. You've covered a lot of information about different web performance optimization techniques. It's time to reflect on the improvements that you've made.

The simple changes you added to the sample application at the end of each chapter gave you better performance scores, but how much did they influence the speed of the site? In order to compare the load times of the application before and after making the optimizations, I uploaded the sample application to a web server and noticed some interesting results. If you would like to test the differences for yourself, please check out the following links:

- Before optimization—http://before.azurewebsites.net/
- After optimization—http://after.azurewebsites.net/

Most of the tests I've been running until now have been against my local machine and didn't simulate a real-world scenario. In order to show the differences between the two samples, I needed to upload them and test them against a real server. I ran both of these websites against the Webpagetest tool and selected a video to highlight differences in load time. The image in figure 12.4 was generated as a side-by-side comparison of the load times of these two sample applications. As you'll notice, the image shows that 1 second into the page load, the optimized version is already showing content to the user. The unoptimized version hasn't shown any content and didn't do so until around 2 seconds in.

Figure 12.5 shows how the optimized version has completed loading at 3.5 seconds, but the unoptimized version isn't close to loading all its content yet!

The unoptimized version of the site takes around 7 seconds to load, while the optimized version completed in 3.5 seconds; this is a remarkable improvement. You can see some even more interesting statistics in table 12.1.

Figure 12.4 A comparison of the optimized sample application versus the unoptimized one. Note that after 1 second, the unoptimized result (top) hasn't even started showing content to the user.

Figure 12.5 The optimized version finished loading within 3.5 seconds, but the unoptimized version (top) is still loading content.

Table 12.1 A detailed comparison of the Surf Store application before any optimizations and after you've applied optimization techniques.

	Before optimization	After optimization
HTTP Requests	24	13
Page Weight	875.72 KB	672.75 KB
Total Load Time	7 seconds	3.5 seconds

I encourage you to try this same test for yourself. The two versions of the website are freely available for you to compare. Fire up www.webpagetest.org and see the differences for yourself. The optimized version of the Surf Store application is a shining example of what a high performance website should be!

If you've been following along with each chapter, you'll have learned how easy it is to transform the load times of your web pages. All the techniques you covered in this book are simple changes you can easily apply to your websites today. There is no better time to start improving your website's speed than now!

appendix

A.1   *Setting up your local machine as a web development server with IIS*

Setting up your local machine to use IIS as a web development server is easy and takes no time at all. Although IIS Express can perform the same tasks that IIS can on a Localhost, many developers prefer to run and debug their websites in a Localhost environment. You no longer need admin access to your machine for web development and setting up virtual directories is a lot easier. This guide will walk you through setting up your local machine to use IIS as a web development server.

Assuming that you have IIS installed on your machine, you'll need to take the following steps to get started:

1. Click Start > Control Panel.
2. Click System and Security > Administrative Tools.
3. In the Administrative Tools window, double-click Internet Information Services (IIS) Manager.

This opens a window similar to the one in figure A.1.

Next, right-click Sites and choose Add Web Site. This opens a window similar to the one in figure A.2.

This window allows you to select a site name as well as set the physical path of your website. Once you've completed these details, click OK and you should be able to start working immediately. Open your web browser, navigate to http://localhost, and you'll be able to see your website!

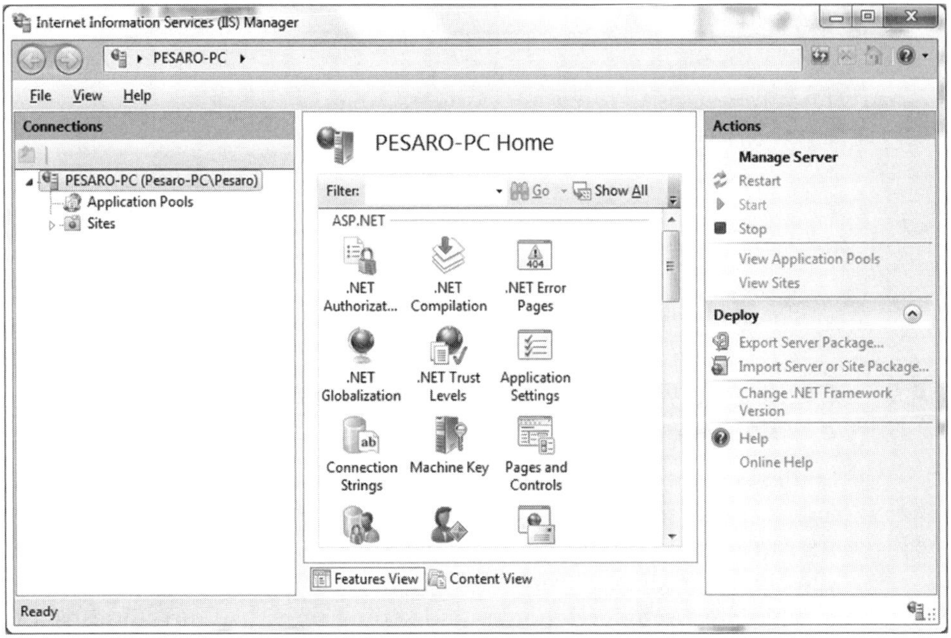

Figure A.1   Internet Information Services (IIS) Manager

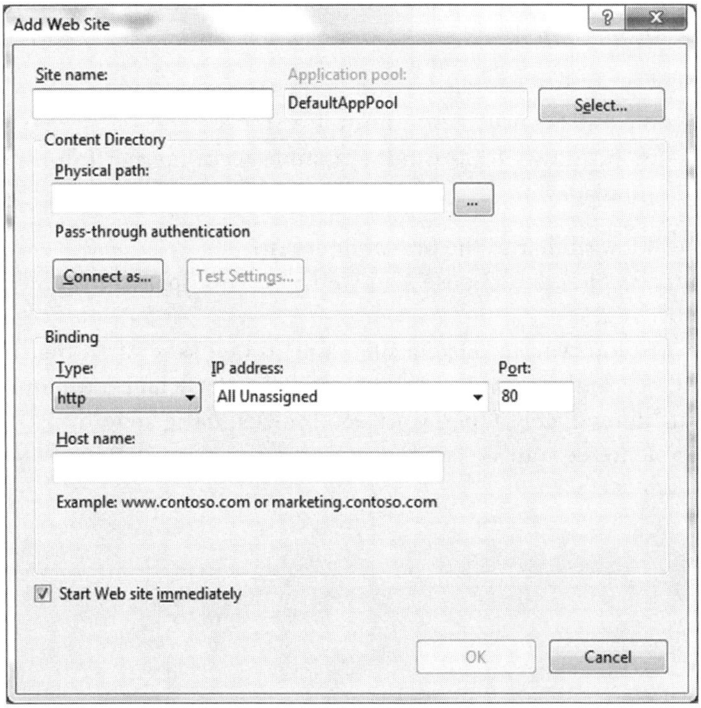

Figure A.2   Set up the site name and physical location of your website.

A.2   *Useful links referenced in this book*

The lists which follow figure A.2 show tools, mentioned throughout the book, used to improve and monitor the performance of your websites.

PROFILING TOOLS

- *Profiling tool*—http://yslow.org/
- *Google PageSpeed tool*—https://developers.google.com/speed/pagespeed/
- *MiniProfiler*—http://miniprofiler.com
- *Online web page profiling*—www.webpagetest.org/
- *Firebug*—www.getfirebug.com
- *HTTPWatch*—www.httpwatch.com/
- *Fiddler*—www.fiddler2.com/fiddler2/

IMAGE OPTIMIZATION TOOLS

- *Smush.it*—http://smush.it/
- *Kraken*—http://kraken.io/
- *Pngcrush*—http://pmt.sourceforge.NET/pngcrush/
- *Jpegtran*—http://jpegclub.org/jpegtran/
- *Visual Studio Extension*—http://mng.bz/2MR6
- *YUI online compressor*—http://refresh-sf.com/yui
- *Online Google Closure compiler*—http://closure-compiler.appspot.com

BEFORE AND AFTER RESULTS

- *Before adding any page optimizations*—http://before.azurewebsites.net/
- *After adding page optimizations in this book*—http://after.azurewebsites.net/

To learn more about managing your IIS server, the Microsoft IIS website is packed with useful resources. Please refer to www.iis.net/learn.

index